T0109486

HIGH SCHOOL FOOTBALL IN CALIFORNIA

Amazing Stories on the Gridiron from San Diego to the Golden Gate and Everywhere In Between

MARK TENNIS

SPORTS
PUBLISHING

Copyright © 2018 by Mark Tennis

All rights reserved. No part of this book may be reproduced in any manner without the express written consent of the publisher, except in the case of brief excerpts in critical reviews or articles. All inquiries should be addressed to Sports Publishing, 307 West 36th Street, 11th Floor, New York, NY 10018.

Sports Publishing books may be purchased in bulk at special discounts for sales promotion, corporate gifts, fund-raising, or educational purposes. Special editions can also be created to specifications. For details, contact the Special Sales Department, Sports Publishing, 307 West 36th Street, 11th Floor, New York, NY 10018 or sportspubbooks@skyhorsepublishing.com.

Sports Publishing® is a registered trademark of Skyhorse Publishing, Inc.®, a Delaware corporation.

Visit our website at www.sportspubbooks.com.

10 9 8 7 6 5 4 3 2 1

Library of Congress Cataloging-in-Publication Data is available on file.

Cover design by Tom Lau
Cover photo credit Roger Clay

ISBN: 978-1-68358-183-3
Ebook ISBN: 978-1-68358-184-0

Printed in the United States of America

For Kathleen Moody
(Wife of 25 years as of August 2018)

For Sean Tennis
(Son & college grad as of May 2018)

CONTENTS

Introduction

Whenever there's a phone call or text or email from Eric Sondheimer of the *Los Angeles Times*, that's a message that has to be checked as soon as possible.

Sondheimer has been a high school sports writer and editor for almost all of the 40 years he's been a journalist. He's definitely earned the label "legendary" and he's probably the best prep sports writer in Southern California history. Twitter and social media have only added to his expertise.

When Eric is on the line, it's often about a state record that needs to be checked. Most of the time he even credits Cal-Hi Sports, which is the service and website I have operated under various ownership since the early years of the internet. Most journalists these days just use our information without any credit.

On a call in January of 2017, Eric wasn't asking about a record. He'd been approached by a publisher in New York to write a book about California high school football. He didn't think he'd have the time and admitted to the publisher that his knowledge of Northern California was limited. He recommended contacting me.

Within a few days, I had been contacted and already was formulating a plan as to how I could complete the manuscript by early February of the following year while still running the Cal-HiSports.com website. If you don't know, having a website is like having a ravenous animal as your pet. You've got to feed it content every day, sometimes twice per day.

I decided the project was going to be worthwhile on many fronts and agreed to do it. My editorial contact at Skyhorse Publishing, Julie Ganz, also gave me a lot of flexibility relating to the book's chapters and what each chapter could be about. Thanks, Julie, for guiding me through the process of becoming an author.

At the beginning, it wasn't going to be a historical book with a decade-by-decade progression of achievements and the development of high school football across the state. There needed to be some history, for sure, but the priority became to shine a spotlight on players, coaches, and even others from outside of the actual playing field. Tell their stories and mix them in with their own voices through numerous interviews.

I didn't get every interview I was hoping for, but got most of them and wasn't going to let the lack of getting an interview deter me from writing the chapter I had in mind.

There was a conscious effort to write one chapter or part of a chapter that would mention players, coaches, or teams from every region of the state. I might have come up a little short for San Diego so apologies up front for that. Many from that area, however, are shown in lists at the back of the book that we are calling "Companion Lists" for many of the chapters. I also may have a little too much from my home base in Stockton, but if you read the chapter on 92-year-old Jack Ferrill, you'll know why I went ahead and wrote it.

Most of the interviews for this book were done in the summer of 2017 with the thinking that many of those I wanted to talk to are quite busy during the actual football season. Fortunately, there were no injuries or other incidents from the 2017 season that caused me to change anything.

There was one team and one individual, however, that were so impressive in the 2017 season that it did create the need to alter two chapters. Then again, those types of stories happen every year.

—MARK TENNIS

Timeline of Key Historical Events

1873—First reported football game or rugby game in the state gets played between Oakland High and the University of California. The game ended in a 0–0 tie when a player reportedly ran into a wooden fence "and was seriously injured."

1891—Amateur Academic Athletic Association formed in San Francisco and Berkeley, the first California high school football league. Oakland and Berkeley were members and are schools that still exist. Boys of San Francisco also was in the league, which later changed its name to Lowell (still exists).

1914—California Interscholastic Federation and CIF Southern Section forms out of Southern California Interscholastic Athletic Council.

1918—Worldwide influenza outbreak causes CIF state playoffs to be canceled. The CIF Southern Section holds its own championship, but the title games aren't until March 8.

1920—In a January matchup billed as the first Southwest American Championship, Long Beach Poly's 1919 CIF state championship team obliterates Phoenix Union (Phoenix, Arizona) 102–0 before 10,000 fans using temporary bleachers at Long Beach Poly.

1923—Bakersfield High wins fourth straight CIF state championship with 27–13 victory over Lick-Wilmerding (San Francisco).

1924—CIF Southern Section votes to skip CIF state playoffs, thereby denying unbeaten Glendale High the chance to win a title. One of Glendale's best players was tackle Marion Morrison, who later became legendary actor John Wayne.

1927—Bakersfield High blanks Fullerton 38–0 to win CIF state football title. It was the last official CIF state championship crowned until 2006.

1935—CIF Los Angeles City Section is formed with Los Angeles Unified School District schools splitting away from the CIF Southern Section.

1942—All California schools greatly curtail their athletic schedules due to the nation's involvement in World War II after Pearl Harbor. There were no football playoffs and most schools only played a handful of football games.

1944—Team of Japanese youngsters having to stay at Camp Manzanar plays Big Pine High in a football game.

1955—California reaches five hundred high schools with football teams. It takes less than fifty more years until that total swells to more than one thousand.

1956—Downey and Anaheim fight to 13–13 tie in the CIF Southern Section championship before 41,393 at the LA Coliseum. That's still the largest crowd to ever witness a non-all-star interscholastic sporting event in state history.

1960—CIF San Diego Section breaks off from CIF Southern Section to form own section. Football playoffs soon follow.

1969—Blair (Pasadena) edges Bishop Amat (La Puente) 28–27 in one of the most memorable CIF Southern Section championship games before 28,169 at the LA Coliseum. The game brought together the Blair Pair—running backs Kermit Johnson and James McAlister—against the pass-catch combo of Pat Haden and John McKay Jr. of Bishop Amat.

1972—CIF Central Coast Section playoffs begin.

1974—CIF North Coast Section playoffs resume. The NCS discontinued playoffs after 1930 and has a longer history than that.

1976—CIF Sac-Joaquin Section playoffs begin.

1979—Cordova (Rancho Cordova) ends season with 102-6-1 record for the decade of the 1970s. It is the best record for the decade in the nation and still one of the best decade records in US prep football history.

1992—De La Salle (Concord) opens the season with 34–14 victory over Merced. The team would not lose again until 2003, setting an all-time national record with 151 consecutive wins.

1992—Bishop Amat (La Puente) defeats Sylmar 31–10 in first and only CIF Bowl, which was an attempt to match the highest class champions from the CIF Southern Section and CIF Los Angeles City Section.

1998—De La Salle (Concord) defeats Mater Dei (Santa Ana) 28–21 before nearly twenty thousand at Angels Stadium. This was perhaps the most significant north-south game played in 60 years since De La Salle already had set the national win streak record and Mater Dei ended as No. 1 team in Southern California.

2000—Tyler Ebell (Ventura) sets state record for rushing yards with 4,495 yards and national record with 64 TDs. It is nearly 1,000 yards above previous state record. National record was broken in 2001.

2001—De La Salle (Concord) defeats Long Beach Poly 29–15 in first-ever matchup of teams ranked No. 1 and No. 2 in the nation at Long Beach Veterans Stadium.

2003—ESPN televises its first-ever high school football game from Diablo Valley College in Pleasant Hill. The opponents were De La Salle (Concord) and Evangel Christian (Shreveport, Louisiana). De La Salle won 27–10 and extended its win streak to 145 games.

2004—Bellevue (Bellevue, Wash.) records 38–20 win over De La Salle (Concord) in Emerald Classic played at Qwest Field in Seattle. That broke the school's all-time national record win streak at 151 games.

2006—CIF resumes state football championships. Three bowl games are played in Carson's Home Depot Center and the first official CIF state champion since 1927 is unbeaten Oaks

Running back Maurice Drew takes handoff from quarterback Matt Gutierrez for De La Salle of Concord during 2001 game against Long Beach Poly. It was the first No. 1 vs. No. 2 matchup of nationally ranked teams in US history. *(Scott Kurtz)*

Christian (Westlake Village). The Lions, however, had to go into overtime to turn back upset-minded Cardinal Newman (Santa Rosa).

2008—CIF adds Open Division to bowl game lineup. Grant (Sacramento) wins first one with 25–20 upset of Long Beach Poly.

2012—CIF adds regional bowl games to bowl game series with the winners facing off in the state bowl games.

2014—Jake Browning (Folsom) sets national record with 229 career TD passes and ties national record with 91 TD passes for 16–0 team. He also passed for state record totals of 5,790 yards (season) and 16,745 yards (career).

2014—CIF drops regional bowl games for Open Division in Northern California and Southern California, but keeps regional bowl games in all other divisions.

2015—CIF changes bowl game format to enable every CIF section champion the opportunity to play in a regional bowl game. The result is 13 divisions with an Open Division remaining at the top of the lineup.

2017—Kazmeir Allen of Tulare sets national record with 72 touchdowns and breaks previous state record of 64 touchdowns set in 2001.

1

Greatest Schools

There are some schools such as Los Angeles High and Berkeley High that had numerous dominating football teams in the early years of the 20th century. Then there are other schools that in the last fifty years have had spectacular eras of success, led by De La Salle High of Concord, and including St. John Bosco of Bellflower, Mater Dei of Santa Ana, and Cordova of Rancho Cordova.

But despite the fact that California has fielded outstanding football teams over the long haul of its history, even some from more than one hundred years ago, the clear leaders of California football are Bakersfield and Long Beach Poly.

Regarding the decision as to which one should be considered the greatest, we'll let alums of the two schools battle it out.

By the end of the 2017 season, when it finished 6–6, Bakersfield had amassed 780 all-time reported wins since its first season of 1896. Long Beach Poly closed the gap with a 9–3 season that put its win total at 767 since its first year of reported scores (1904). No other school in state history is even getting close to 700.

Those wins for Bakersfield, however, include rugby during the early 1910s when rugby was played as a substitute sport for football. That's believed to be a total of 12 wins. Long Beach Poly never played rugby in those years, so if one looks at the Cal-Hi Sports state records and considers most all-time wins not including rugby, then Bakersfield's total is 768 and Long Beach Poly is right behind at 767.

Those win totals for both schools don't include forfeit wins or forfeit losses. Bakersfield also has two World War II seasons—in 1943 and 1944—in which there were two varsity teams and no wins have ever been counted for those years because it has never been verified which team was "varsity" or "official" and which team was not.

Bakersfield Drillers

Other than simply having more wins than any school in California history, the Drillers stand alone for being the only school with two different head coaches who have won more than 200 games.

The first was Dwight "Goldie" Griffith, who began in 1908 and guided the teams until 1942, and then once more in 1945. Griffith could be called the state's first legendary football coach and finished with 207 wins, just 50 losses, and 27 ties. Playoff games were not as plentiful in those days, but Bakersfield was the dominant team in the first era of CIF state playoffs from 1919 to 1927 when it won the title six times in those years.

Griffith's 1927 team, which was the reigning CIF state champion for 78 years since the next one wasn't crowned until 2006, is still regarded as one of the greatest the state has ever seen. The Drillers won the state title with a 38–0 demolition of Fullerton and had wins that year over college freshmen teams from Fresno State and Whittier College.

Paul Briggs was the second of those coaches to reach 200 wins or more. He was a mountain of a man at 6-foot-5 but had a gentle touch and went 209–99–12 from 1953 to 1985.

"They were big boys and they were fast boys," said CIF Central Section historian Bob Barnett in a 2017 interview. "The only competition they had in the 1920s and 1930s was from Wasco [a much smaller community]. But they had a good system going and had great coaching. They have kept it going for so long."

Kern County, which had a population of nearly nine hundred thousand in 2015, only had one high school for the city of Bakersfield until 1937 and it was Bakersfield High.

"They have had big enrollments for most of the time [the team has] been great," Barnett said. "But you can say the same thing about Long Beach Poly."

The Drillers, led by head coach Paul Golla, added a seventh CIF state title in 2013 when they sped past Del Oro of Loomis 56–26 in the Division I championship. The CIF also has counted a 1916 title for Bakersfield's total, but that title was from a declaration by the CIF Federated Council at the time and was not a win on the field. Cal-Hi Sports only counts wins on the field, so for its state record book the total is seven. Cal-Hi Sports also lists San Diego High as its 1916 State Team of the Year. After the 2017 CIF state championships, the only other school with seven titles was De La Salle.

Another state record that Bakersfield owns is for most CIF section titles, with 37. The Drillers also have a streak of winning 10 straight league titles (1992–2001) and a streak of appearing in postseason playoffs for 31 straight seasons.

Bakersfield's most famous football alum is NFL Hall of Famer Frank Gifford, who is even more well-known as a broadcaster.

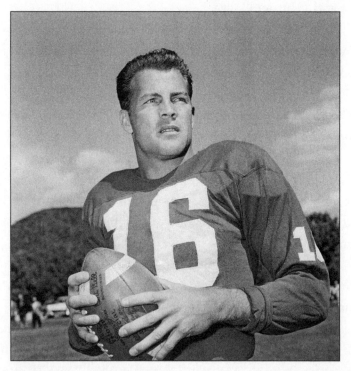

The most famous alum of Bakersfield is NFL Hall of Famer Frank Gifford. *(Associated Press)*

He died in 2015 at the age of eighty-four, but in 2013 when the Drillers were in the state finals, Gifford's wife, Kathie Lee, was reportedly following score updates on Twitter and keeping him in the loop.

Other prominent NFL players from Bakersfield over the years have been running back Theo Bell, linebacker Jeff Siemen, defensive back Louis Wright, and defensive back Michael Stewart.

In the 2017 season, after the Drillers didn't play there in 2016, Griffith Field (named for the legendary coach)—their home stadium for many years—was reopened after a multi-million-dollar upgrade.

Long Beach Poly Jackrabbits

Piling up more than 700 all-time wins doesn't get Poly fans the most excited and most prideful when talking about their school. It's not even close.

It's this fact and this fact only: No high school in America has had more players achieve NFL status. The exact all-time total varies when you count practice squads, but it's more than fifty (probably closer to sixty), and there are Poly grads getting drafted and then becoming new stars in the NFL just about every year.

In 2017, wide receiver JuJu Smith-Schuster of the Pittsburgh Steelers joined the party. Wide receiver/kick returner Kaelin Clay of the Carolina Panthers also made an impact. Other more recent Jackrabbits starring in the league have been wide receiver DeSean Jackson, tight end Marcedes Lewis, and defensive lineman Jurrell Casey.

Many of those NFL players from Poly continue to stay connected to their school for many years.

Former All-Pro and three-time Super Bowl winner Willie McGinest of the New England Patriots still helps coach current Poly players and offers them guidance.

Although Long Beach Poly didn't win in this CIF Division I state final in 2012 against Granite Bay, wide receiver JuJu Smith made this touchdown catch. JuJu was one of the top rookie receivers in the NFL in 2017 going by JuJu Smith-Schuster. *(Scott Kurtz)*

"I'm always bragging about being from Poly," McGinest once said in an interview. "The way I brag you'd think the world stopped and ended at Long Beach Poly."

McGinest touched on one reason why the Jackrabbits have been a California powerhouse not just in football for more than 100 years but also in many other sports, particularly track and field.

"Race was not an issue there," he commented. "It's just an atmosphere in which the staff really cares about everyone and puts in a lot of overtime, especially for the student-athlete."

JoJo Wicker, a defensive lineman standout at Arizona State in 2017, is one of those with whom McGinest has worked.

"A lot of people from there have helped me," Wicker said at the 2017 Pac-12 Conference media day. "They've been there, done that. They have a lot of knowledge.

"It was a blue-collar mentality and they taught ways to maintain the body. And yes, it does build up as the generations go on. I will do the same."

Going back a few years before McGinest was drafted in the first round in 1994 by the Patriots, Poly grad Leonard Russell was selected in the first round in 1991 also by the Patriots, and the year before that in 1990 the Chicago Bears selected Poly grad Mark Carrier in the first round as well. Both Carrier and Russell also were NFL Rookies of the Year for 1991 and 1992.

Looking back even further, the Jackrabbits' greatest influence in the NFL has been at the wide receiver position. Gene Washington (San Francisco 49ers), Tony Hill (Dallas Cowboys), Stephone Paige (Kansas City Chiefs), Bobby Morris (Chicago Bears), and Earl McCullough (Detroit Lions) are all among the best receivers their NFL teams have ever had.

Four players from Poly's 2001 team (regarded as one of the top two teams in school history) earned NFL playing time, led by Marcedes Lewis. The other three have been linemen Winston Justice and Manuel Wright and defensive back Darnell Bing. That Jackrabbit squad, which also became the first in the nation to have five *Parade* magazine All-Americans and had 28 players on the roster play for Division I colleges, won its third straight CIF Southern Section title. The only reason Poly wasn't unbeaten is because it lost a game to what many believe is the best team De La Salle of Concord has ever had.

Poly's other team that in 2015 was ranked third on a list of the state's all-time greatest teams was the squad coached in 1959 by Dave Levy. That Jackrabbit squad ended 11–0, won its second straight CIF Southern Section top division crown, and was described in one press report as "having the top four running backs in Southern California." State Player of the Year Willie Brown, a running back, was the leader of that team.

The Jackrabbits don't have close to the number of CIF state titles as Bakersfield. They did win the very first one in 1919, but have gone 0–2 in their only appearances during the modern-day CIF state finals that started in 2006.

The school's other state record book listings are for consecutive league titles (17 from 1992 to 2008), section titles (19), and most consecutive section playoff appearances (35 from 1980 to 2014). None of those totals, however, are state records.

Poly has a huge edge on Bakersfield looking at it from an NFL player perspective, but the Drillers have higher totals in other categories, especially wins.

2

The Road to State

—————

Whether it's from signs taped to the bleachers, painted on the side of a bus, or tagged on a team's social media platform, the phrase "Road to State" can be seen referring to teams of all shapes and sizes as the playoffs get underway each fall.

Today, the California Interscholastic Federation presents state championship trophies in 13 divisions with an Open Division at the top in which the very best team from Northern California plays the very best from Southern California regardless of school size and then in 12 divisions determined by a competitive equity formula.

If that sounds complicated, it is. But for this book there's a different "Road to State," and that's the road that was taken by the CIF itself.

In the early years of the CIF, starting in 1915, there were state championships not only in football but also in other sports like baseball, basketball, track & field, and swimming. Those events began to dissipate in the early 1920s for various reasons, and then after 1927 the CIF state football championships were halted.

For more than 70 years from 1927 to approximately 1997, there wasn't even much discussion about CIF state football games. Sure, in the 1970s when Cordova of Rancho Cordova (near Sacramento) had some super teams that appeared would be superior or equal to the best of Southern California, there were some who wondered what a revised CIF state playoff system might be like. But nothing close to a proposal was ever made.

Perhaps the first attempt was a proposed series of bowl games published by Cal-Hi Sports in the 1980s in which founder Nelson Tennis came up with a Gold Bowl for Class 4A teams, a Silver Bowl for Class 3A, a Bronze Bowl for Class 2A, an Aluminum Bowl for Class 1A, and a Redwood Bowl for Class B. None of those proposals, however, dealt with any of the logistics about travel and teams that may have had to play 17 games. It was done primarily to stir debate.

The CIF itself also began to grow its own lineup of state championship events. The CIF state track meet never did go away and continues to thrive in its new home venue of Veterans Stadium in Clovis. A CIF state meet for wrestling was added in 1973 and was followed by boys golf (1976), girls volleyball (1978), girls golf (1978), boys basketball (1980), girls basketball (1981), and boys and girls cross country (1987).

Debates about which team should be ranked No. 1 in the final Cal-Hi Sports state rankings and highest among California teams in *USA Today* then began to ramp up in the 1990s. Part of that debate was fueled by the dominance displayed in Northern California by the program at De La Salle of Concord. But it wasn't just De La Salle. In the final state rankings for the 1992 season, the top six slots were occupied by undefeated teams De La Salle (13–0), Bishop Amat of La Puente (15–0), St. Francis of Mountain View (13–0), Clovis West of Fresno (13–0), Morse of San Diego (14–0), and Los Alamitos (13–0–1).

For most of the years between 1927 and into the 1990s before De La Salle came along, it was almost an unwritten rule for most media groups doing national rankings that whichever team won the CIF Southern Section top divisional title would automatically be considered the de-facto state champion. While that was true for more years than not, simply ignoring the rest of the state just wasn't fair and it was the lazy approach as well.

De La Salle wasn't State Team of the Year until 1992 and then began its national record win streak that lasted until 2004. In 1998 and beyond, the Spartans also began to actively schedule many of the best teams from Southern California. They went 4–0 against Mater Dei of Santa Ana, which was *USA Today*'s national champion in 1994 and 1996, and also 2–0 against Long Beach Poly.

The CIF itself doesn't credit this interest in De La Salle during its streak years as a factor for a growing interest in CIF state football championships, but for many fans of the top programs in the state that was clearly the case.

Getting A Proposal To Pass

The CIF Federated Council is where all proposals to change rules or add state championship events get passed and become reality, or it's where they go to die.

Before a new event or new rule is passed, however, each of the 10 sections in the state that have their own board of managers conducts a vote instructing its delegates on the CIF Federated Council how to vote. Therefore, before almost all actions that are taken by the CIF Federated Council, a canvass of those section votes usually provides the answer as to how a particular issue is going to be decided.

There was a proposal for a series of CIF football bowl games that matched teams from different corners of the state against each other in the late 1990s under then-CIF executive director Jack Hayes that failed. But there remained a solid core of CIF section commissioners and others within the CIF state office that didn't give up on the idea.

One of those was CIF Sac-Joaquin Section commissioner Pete Saco. He had begun his career in educational athletics as a coach at Lodi High and at Tokay High in Lodi in the fall of 1977. By 1979, Saco had become the varsity boys basketball coach at Lodi and then in 1981 he was named the school's athletic director. From 1981 until 1993, Saco served in both roles. At that time, longtime section commissioner Clarke Coover retired. Saco applied for the job and was hired.

Despite the football proposal failing several years earlier, the CIF state office was still in an expansion mode to add state championship events and in 2002 the Federated Council adopted a series of guidelines by which all new proposals for state championships needed to abide.

"I had gotten frustrated with the process, and can remember clearly after that meeting talking with incoming CIF President Charley Berger, who was from our section, and told him, 'You know what we need is a football proposal,'" Saco remembered. "He looked at me and said, 'Then you should be the one to put it together.'"

That proposal began to take shape the next day when Berger, Sac-Joaquin Section assistant commissioner John Williams, and Saco went golfing. The following January at the Sac-Joaquin Section Board of Managers meeting, Saco felt he needed the support of that board for him to move forward.

"They said, 'Fine. You can do it. We just don't want the season cut short. The schools have to keep their 10-game regular seasons,'" Saco said.

Saco and Williams weren't able to really get serious about their proposal until later in the spring of 2004, which came after their own busy winter championship season.

"A lot of what we laid out way back then is still in play," Saco said. "We felt that only section winners should be allowed to play in these games and that there would be a committee to select the teams."

By this time, the CIF state office was under the direction of executive director Marie Ishida, who was a strong supporter of the state football proposal. The CIF also was getting responses from potential sponsors, who indicated they didn't want to commit to anything unless football was being added soon.

Still, there remained significant opposition. Saco and Williams knew that the massive CIF Southern Section, which actually has more schools in it than every state in the nation other than Texas, Florida, Illinois, Ohio, and New York, was probably never going to vote for it.

The final proposal ended up calling for three games to be played on one day—Division I, Division II, and Division III—with those divisions determined by school enrollment and also for a committee of CIF section commissioners to choose the teams. With other provisions included such as the one in which only section champions could be eligible, the vote was close but it passed in 2005 at the fall meeting of the Federated Council. The commissioners met after the 2005 section championships to hold a mock vote of what the games would look like, and then in 2006 the first such games were played.

As expected, most of the controversy surrounding those early games was about which teams were chosen to play. De La Salle was an easy choice for the north in Division I for that first year, but the best teams in the south based on enrollment were actually in Division II (Orange Lutheran) and Division III (Oaks Christian of Westlake Village). The committee chose Canyon of Canyon Country, a team with two losses, to face De La Salle in Division I and ended up beating the Spartans.

After De La Salle won the Division I state title in 2007, the 2008 format of the bowl games was altered to add an Open Division at the top plus a game at the bottom, for small schools, for a two-day series of games. The selection of teams for that 2008 Open Division was very difficult, especially in the north where there were three teams, including De La Salle plus Grant of Sacramento and Bellarmine of San Jose, vying for two berths. Grant won the vote of the commissioners after several 5–5 verdicts, with De La Salle getting the Division I game and Bellarmine getting left out.

As the games began to gain in stature, more changes to the format were voted in. For the 2012 bowl games, a Northern California and Southern California regional game was added, including the Open Division. By 2014, the Open Division for each region was eliminated (teams now just take one week off before playing) but there remained the problem of outstanding teams being left on the sidelines.

After the section commissioners voted to choose San Diego Madison for one of its divisional slots in 2012 and did not choose unbeaten Wasco, the cries of protest from the Wasco community in Kern County were heard even at the state capitol.

"I thought to myself at the time that before I retired, I've got to come up with something to get everybody invited," Saco recalled. "And it wasn't just the teams at the top. We'd have many teams each year you'd see on the board that were section champions that were never going to be considered the way it was set up."

To guarantee that every CIF section champion would have at least a regional bowl game became a process comparable to solving a 5,000-piece jigsaw puzzle. The format couldn't have all champions from the Central Section, LA City Section, San Diego Section, and Southern Section considered in the south region because there would be too many teams compared to the north. In the end, the puzzle was solved by coming up with a protocol in which three teams from the Central Section would move to the north side of the bracket with three teams from that section staying in the south. The CIF also had to use two play-in games on the north bracket to make it all fit.

While there are legitimate concerns about too many teams playing 16 games in a season and there are some divisions that the competition is indeed watered down compared to the top two or three divisions, the 13-division format implemented for the 2015 season gives many more schools and its players the experience of winning CIF state titles.

This CIF state championship trophy from 2016 was captured by Sierra Canyon of Chatsworth. *(James K. Leash/SportStars)*

In 2016, this included Paraclete of Lancaster becoming the first school from the Antelope Valley to win a state title in addition to two teams winning titles from the City of Oakland—Bishop O'Dowd and McClymonds. The city needed a celebration after O'Dowd and McClymonds won state titles. It came just two weeks after the Ghost Ship warehouse fire killed 36 people.

In 2017, Bishop Diego of Santa Barbara became the first school from Santa Barbara County to win a state title and it was a breakthrough year for the city of San Francisco when Galileo High won the Division 6-A championship.

"I think it's fantastic," CIF executive director Roger Blake said during an interview at halftime of the 2017 CIF Open Division championship. "We've got really exciting games being played all over the state. We've got games in Calexico and El Centro and here [Sacramento]. It's a once in a lifetime experience for these kids."

Blake and CIF associate executive director Ron Nocetti (who directs the state football playoff event) also are happy that using competitive equity to place teams into divisions reduces the chances of blowouts in both the regional and state final contests.

"You look at the scores right now and there's just two blowouts," Blake said. "How it's progressed from three games and then five and then to now it's still just section champions who are playing. We've got a couple of runner-ups, but those are from Open Divisions and we have to let the sections decide that."

In the future, it's hard to fathom many changes to the format because all section champions as of the 2017 season are in these CIF games. Saco does see possibilities in the Open Division such as having the top two teams in the north and south going in but playing in a cross-bracket doubleheader, a big event that TV and other sponsors might like. He also would like to look into possibilities of Open Division teams being able to drop back down into the Division I bracket if they were to lose in a first-round game. That would be more for other sports, however, and not so much football.

"There's always going to continue to be tweaks to the system," Saco replied. "The good thing about [2016] is that almost all of the state championship games were very good football games. That's what's really trying to be created."

3

Greatest Teams

An all-time great high school football team is like a fine wine. It ages with the passage of time.

That is why it doesn't make sense to declare any team, no matter what it has accomplished at the end of a current season, the best or greatest ever.

It takes time to find out how many of the best players on the best teams develop in their careers. And it's not just the development of those players on the top team in question, but also the players on the teams that were defeated along the way.

If a team that was dominant and unbeaten with a CIF state title can be viewed in retrospect 10 or 15 years after it played, for example, and had a Super Bowl-winning quarterback with two or three other top NFL players, then that team should move up for consideration amongst the all-time greatest. Conversely, if that team ended up with zero NFL players, then perhaps that team moves down a notch or two.

And before going any further in identifying the greatest teams in California prep football history, notice the word "greatest" as opposed to "best." When considering a team from twenty, thirty, or fifty years ago, when physical training wasn't as advanced and when offensive systems were not as well developed, then it's obvious that in actual player-to-player comparisons the newer teams would likely win easily if any of these teams were to play each other. By using the term "greatest," that means historical achievement, that means how much better a team was than its contemporary competition, and perhaps that means a team that represents a series of other top teams from several seasons in a row.

Looking at each school's list of historically significant teams over the years also is an important consideration. What is the greatest or best team that school has ever had? Which one should be second, third, etc.?

Each season's final state and national rankings need to be evaluated as well. As it currently stands any team essentially can claim a mythical national title by being ranked by only one media entity. If *USA Today* picks your team and no other group does, it doesn't matter. Even if it's just the MaxPreps computer rankings and your team isn't No. 1 by *USA Today*, Football America, the National Prep Poll, and the MaxPreps Xcellent 25 or anything else, it doesn't matter. If somebody or a computer out there shows your team at No. 1, then printing national champion t-shirts can be done.

All-time great teams generally all have a mythical national title attached to them as well as being No. 1 in the final Cal-Hi Sports state rankings. That doesn't mean that a No. 2 team in the state can't be considered an all-time great team. It's just that the No. 2 team will forever be behind the No. 1 team. The only time that hasn't been the case was for one of De La Salle's many undefeated No. 1 teams (1996), listed behind one of the two Mater Dei of Santa Ana teams that was ranked No. 1 nationally by *USA Today*.

The ten teams featured below represent the best teams at those particular schools as well as different decades. They are not presented in any particular order or ranking. Teams from Long Beach Poly and Bakersfield were highlighted in an earlier chapter and teams from Mission Viejo, Folsom, Centennial of Corona, El Toro of Lake Forest, El Rancho of Pico Rivera, and Fontana are highlighted in later chapters. *Note: For rankings of the state's all-time Top 25 teams, see companion lists at the back of this book.*

2017 Mater Dei Monarchs (15–0)

Head coach Bruce Rollinson, who looks like he walked out of an old Western movie with a thick mustache and a scruffy voice, had been careful throughout the 2017 season whenever a reporter asked him to compare the team at Mater Dei High of Santa Ana to any others he had in his previous 28 seasons at the school.

All the buffers were removed after the Monarchs completed a 15–0 season with a convincing 52–21 victory over De La Salle of Concord in the CIF Open Division state championship on a cold, windy night at Sacramento State's Hornet Stadium.

"When you look at it now and now that it's over, I can say it and that is that this is the best football team I've had in my tenure," Rollinson said in a TV interview. "I can't even describe how happy I am for these guys. To go 15 straight games and play like we did every time. Now we can say we're national champions."

The state title, combined with two wins over state No. 2 St. John Bosco of Bellflower (with the final one securing the CIF Southern Section Division I championship) plus a significant win in September over national powerhouse Bishop Gorman of Las Vegas that ended that program's 55-game win streak, added up for Mater Dei to be No. 1 in final national rankings by Max-Preps, *USA Today*, and other media groups.

The Monarchs had been No. 1 before in *USA Today*'s final rankings, having had undefeated teams in 1994 and 1996. Yet they did not secure every victory so easily. The 1994 team had to win one playoff game after recovering an onside kick in the closing seconds, and the 1996 team also had a few close calls.

For Mater Dei in 2017, there was little drama. In the team's first matchup with St. John Bosco, the Braves had a chance to cut the lead to a one-score margin in the fourth quarter, but a field goal attempt was blocked. The Monarchs wound up winning 31–21 and that was their closest game of the season.

As with many all-time great teams, what happened the previous season was a big factor for the Monarchs. They were a team loaded with mostly juniors and sophomores and were rolling along as the top-ranked team in the nation when they lost to St. John Bosco 42–28 in the CIFSS D1 championship after previously beating the Braves two months earlier. That loss was on the players' minds every time they took the field in 2017.

"We were playing for the seniors from last year," said 6-foot-7, 320-pound offensive lineman Tommy Brown. "We just remembered that loss and didn't want it to happen again."

Head coach Bruce Rollinson from Mater Dei of Santa Ana waves to the crowd after team won CIF Open Division title in 2017 and capped perfect season. *(Willie Eashman)*

Brown, one of several members of the offensive line who pushed 300 pounds, protected junior quarterback JT Daniels. Daniels had been named the Gatorade National Player of the Year three days after the De La Salle win and in January was selected as the Cal-Hi Sports Mr. Football State Player of the Year. Though he didn't have quite the same passing numbers as a junior that he did as a sophomore, Daniels was much improved in all facets of his development, including his quickness as a runner. Daniels finished the season with 4,123 yards passing and 52 touchdown passes, and he rushed for another 559 yards with nine more scores.

Several days after the Gatorade ceremony, Daniels made news again when he reclassified so that he could graduate in June of 2018 as a senior and then attend USC in the fall of 2018. If he had been playing in 2018 for Mater Dei, Daniels was on pace to establish several state career passing records.

For Daniels, however, the success of the season for himself and the team was more about a consistent approach to every game and not so much about redemption.

"I haven't thought much about it to be honest since January," he said during an interview earlier in the season while walking off the field at Levi's Stadium in Santa Clara. "We haven't been worried about last year. It's just been about taking the mistakes we've made and how we learn from them."

Amon-Ra St. Brown was the team's leading receiver and most dangerous playmaker in the open field. Ranked as the state's No. 1 college prospect for the Class of 2018 by many college recruiting services (but slipping behind his teammate Daniels after that reclassification), St. Brown missed three early-season games with an injury but still caught 72 passes for 1,320 yards and 20 TDs.

Three others that Daniels often threw to also created mismatches in single coverage by opposing defenses. Seniors Nick

Remigio and Chris Parks and junior Horace "Bru" McCoy all caught at least 45 passes for at least 700 yards and combined for 26 touchdowns.

The defense wasn't too shabby, either. The linebacker duo of Solomon Tuliaupupu and Mase Funa was so impressive that many from Southern California have never seen a better one. Linebacker Jack Genova was the leading tackler against De La Salle while defensive end Nathan Logoleo led the team in sacks with 17.

Orange County Register prep columnist Steve Fryer watched the Monarchs in several of their biggest games and was more than impressed.

"I've never seen a team like this," said Fryer, who has had a forty-year career covering games in Southern California, as many of the Monarchs were still exchanging hugs with each other. "They played relaxed but with a purpose. They had a fun, silly side but got down to business when it was game time."

2001 De La Salle Spartans (12–0)

With its 151-game win streak from 1992 to 2004 that included six No. 1 national ranking finishes and broke the previous national record for longest win streak by more than double, a De La Salle team from that era was probably going to be amongst the greatest. But which one?

The 2001 edition of the Spartans makes the most sense. The primary reason is that this team probably beat the best team that De La Salle has ever played—Long Beach Poly of 2001 (see Chapter One)—and it was a team that had the best quarterback in school history in Matt Gutierrez, as well as the best running back in school history in Maurice Drew.

Both Gutierrez and Drew played in the NFL, and Drew (he later changed his last name to Jones-Drew) led the NFL in rushing twice for the Jacksonville Jaguars. This DLS team also had another future NFL player, defensive tackle Derek Landri, who was so dominant as a two-way lineman for the Spartans that he was the 2001 Mr. Football State Player of the Year.

Early in the season, the Spartans ventured to Clovis to play Buchanan, which won the CIF Central Section title the year before, and beat the Bears 56–14. They next took on Mater Dei of Santa Ana (the only team to beat Long Beach Poly in that school's dominating five-year run in Southern California) and hammered the Monarchs, 34–6, to complete a 4–0 sweep of that school that had begun in 1998.

In none of those games, and even in a 42–0 blanking of Mountain View St. Francis, head coach Bob Ladouceur barely used Drew. Instead, he sprung Drew against the Jackrabbits. In the first ever No. 1 vs. No. 2 game for teams in the national rankings and a matchup that generated credential requests from the *New York Times* and other national publications, Drew scored four times as the Spartans won at Veterans Memorial Stadium in Long Beach, 29–15.

De La Salle continued to accumulate the easy wins, then in the CIF North Coast Section final on a rainy night at Diablo Valley College, faced 11–0 San Leandro. This was the third straight year that San Leandro went into an NCS final at 11–0, and this time the Pirates had two players—quarterback Dennis Dixon and defensive back Jarrad Page—who would later become starters in the NFL. It still made no difference. Drew rushed for 156 yards on 14 carries and scored three times as the Spartans won 48–13.

There were other De La Salle teams that arguably had more talent than in 2001, especially those in 1998 and 1999 that had Mr. Football State Player of the Year D. J. Williams on them, and the

Spartans also had a super-talented team in 2003 that put the win streak total at 151. That 2003 team included linebacker/tight end Terrence Kelly, who was going to play at the University of Oregon before he was murdered after a pickup basketball game in Richmond.

But of all the championship teams in the De La Salle era, the 2001 squad is the one that probably best represents all of the attributes of the program.

After that last game, Ladouceur said the team was not the most talented he'd ever had, but was tied for being the best due to its consistency. Defensive coordinator Terry Eidson added that it was the best defensive line in school history.

There were indeed a few other DLS teams more talented (mainly because 1999 Mr. Football D. J. Williams wasn't on the 2001 team), but the 2001 team may best represent all that the program is known for.

1954 Vallejo Apaches (9–0)*

This team has unquestionably aged well over the years like a wine from nearby Vallejo in the Napa Valley.

In fact, in the days before there were even CIF section playoffs in Northern California and when there were no CIF state play-offs or bowl games (1927 to 2006) at all, there has perhaps never been a team in state history so much better than its contemporary competition than this one.

For the 1954 season in Northern California, the No. 2 ranked team was 8–1 Lodi, which suffered its only loss to Vallejo by a whopping 40–7 margin. The Apaches also handed longtime Berkeley coach Fred Moffett his worst loss, a 41–0 defeat of the Yellowjackets.

Senior running back Dick Bass was the team's star player and he went on to star for more than ten years in the NFL. But Bass was not Vallejo's only standout. Fullback D. L. Hurd played for the Baltimore Colts, receiver/kick returner Bob Coronado played for the Pittsburgh Steelers, and defensive end Ron Stover was drafted by the NFL but played professionally in Canada. Junior quarterback Norman Bass (Dick's younger brother) also became the first African-American two-sport pro athlete (MLB, NFL) in the years following Jackie Robinson's historic breakthrough. Senior quarterback Tom Zunino didn't go to the NFL, but did become one of the winningest head coaches in Northern California history at Vacaville.

After the Apaches defeated Tamalpais of Mill Valley 87–25, head coach Bill McGowan of Santa Rosa said: "Without a doubt, the Apaches have the greatest team in prep school history and we know they could run up 70 or 80 points against us with no trouble at all."

In back-to-back games, Bass had 12 carries for 327 yards and five touchdowns against Salinas (77–12 win) and then eight carries for 395 yards and four scores against Drake of San Anselmo (52–0 win). He ended the season with 1,964 yards and 37 TDs on just 133 carries (a 14.8 yards per carry average).

There was so much interest in the team at the time that the University of Pacific did something perhaps never tried before or since: It offered scholarships to the entire Vallejo team.

Four years later, with Bass starring at UOP and many of his former Vallejo High teammates also playing for the Tigers, they upset Cal 24–20 and that Cal team was the last one from Berkeley to play in the Rose Bowl.

Vallejo's other victories in 1954 were against McClymonds of Oakland (47–6), Napa (53–0), Riordan of San Francisco (52–0), and Santa Rosa (39–7).

*Note: Vallejo is no longer the Apaches. The school changed its nickname to Redhawks in 2014.

1969 Blair Vikings (13–0)

One of the most prominent national high school football historians is the late Barry Sollenberger of Arizona, who once proclaimed the Blair High of Pasadena squad of 1969 one of the nation's dozen greatest of the 20th century.

Head coach Pete Yoder directed a squad led by future pro running backs James McAlister (228 points)—the Mr. Football State Player of the Year—and Kermit Johnson (158 points). The duo, arguably the best running back tandem in state history, combined for 4,082 yards rushing and 53 touchdowns to help Blair pile up 580 points, including 62 in a 62–7 whitewashing of rival Muir.

The Vikings also get major credit for winning one of the best CIF section finals in state history, a 28–27 win over Bishop Amat of La Puente before 28,169 fans at the Los Angeles Coliseum. Bishop Amat featured quarterback Pat Haden and receiver John McKay Jr., who later became standouts at USC.

The memorable game almost never happened, as Lakewood took a 19–18 lead early in the fourth period in the section semifinals, and with 35 seconds remaining, Blair had the ball on its own 3-yard line. Things looked bleak, especially with starting quarterback Ken Lipkin out with injury. On the next play, Charles Phillips (a future NFL defensive back) took the snap, rolled out in the end zone, and threw a pass to tight end Eugene Jones. He caught the ball on the Blair 35-yard line, juked several defenders, and went in for a 97-yard touchdown to give Blair the improbable 24–19 win.

Known as the Blair Pair, Johnson and McAlister led the Vikings to easier wins earlier in the playoffs against Hueneme of Oxnard (62–0) and Santa Monica (44–19). In its final regular season outing, Blair blasted Crescenta Valley of La Crescenta 58–22.

2013 St. John Bosco Braves (16–0)

When this team ended the four-year run of Concord De La Salle as the CIF Open Division champion and became the first school in the state to go 16–0 in the highest CIF division, many long-time Southern California observers said it was possibly the most complete team they'd ever seen. For offense, defense, or special teams, there was just no weakness.

Cal-Hi Sports State Junior of the Year Josh Rosen and State Sophomore of the Year Sean McGrew led the offense. Rosen (who started as a true freshman at UCLA and could be headed for a long career in the NFL), passed for 3,200 yards and 39 TDs and rushed for nearly 600 yards. Against De La Salle, he was 12 of 17 passing for 200 yards and two TDs and rushed seven times for 69 yards. McGrew wasn't a starter early in the season, but quickly emerged as a breakaway running back. He ended with 2,076 yards rushing and 21 TDs, including his spectacular 17-carry, 372-yard, 6-TD outing in a 70–49 win over Corona Centennial in the Southern California Open Division bowl game.

The senior class was among the most talented in California in many years. Offensive lineman Damian Mama (USC), DB Jaleel Wadood (UCLA), WR Shay Fields (Colorado), and DB Naijiel Hale already were getting starts as true freshmen in the Pac-12, although Hale later left Washington.

Some of the Braves' other wins in 2013 were against Chandler of Arizona (52–31), Mater Dei of Santa Ana twice (24–2 and 34–7), Crenshaw of Los Angeles (75–35), and Alemany of Mission Hills (56–15).

Head coach Jason Negro started building a national

Head coach Jason Negro from St. John Bosco of Bellflower has built power-house program, including a 2013 team that went 16-0 and won CIF Open Division state title. *(Mark Tennis)*

championship-contending program at the school in 2010. By 2012, the Braves had a team with Rosen starting as a sophomore that was 12–0 before losing a playoff game to Long Beach Poly. After 2013, Negro's program continued to flourish with a second CIF Open Division state title in 2016. The top player from the 2016 team, 6-foot-5, 320-pound offensive lineman Wyatt Davis, was the Mr. Football State Player of the Year.

1993 Eisenhower Eagles (14–0)

If someone were to ask to pick the best team ever seen in person for one game, the way that the Eagles played on a December night at Anaheim Stadium in 1993 may very well be that team.

Eisenhower took on a Mater Dei of Santa Ana squad that it had lost to in 1990 and 1991 and put on a display of offense, defense, special teams, and everything in between for a 56–3 win in the CIF Southern Section major division championship.

The 56-point total was still a record for the CIFSS's top division until 2015 and the margin is still one of the highest for any division. The Eagles were leading 35–3 at halftime and the only negatives on the night were a 5-yard penalty and a meaningless interception.

Option quarterback Glenn Thompkins and running back Marlon Farlow, who rushed for 200 yards and three touchdowns versus the Monarchs, led the Eisenhower offense. Receiver Julius McChristian got the rout going with an interception on Mater Dei's first series and later scored on a 48-yard pass reception.

Another reason the Eagles were special is that the 1993 team capped a four-year run in which head coach Tom Hoak guided the program to a 48–4–1 record. The '93 team was not No. 1 in the nation (No. 2 by most), but in 1990 and in 1991 the Eagles were *USA Today*'s No. 1 team until their losses to the Monarchs.

1971 Carson Colts (12–0)

The late Gene Vollnogle is one of the greatest coaches in state history and this was his greatest team. This edition of the Colts also is considered the top team ever from the LA City Section and was one of the most talented, balanced (offense and defense) units in Southern California history.

The Colts had speed on the outside led by wide receiver Wesley Walker, State Junior of the Year, and a powerful running game led by Jimmy Vaipou. Walker would later star in the NFL for the New York Jets.

The defense, which included linebacker Brad Vaughn, linebacker Marvin Morris, defensive back Danny Kay, defensive back

Sam Harper, and Walker, put up numbers that are unmatched in state history. The unit forced an incredible 74 turnovers (a state record), including 41 fumble recoveries—a state record by a wide margin and reportedly No. 2 on the all-time US prep list.

When coaches talk about "11 hats on the ball," 16mm film of this team is what they should be showing. The Colts defeated rival Banning of Wilmington, 29–28, in one of the greatest regular season games in state history and outscored opponents 483–147.

Carson, which often performed a Samoan War Dance before its games in a ritual that many other schools throughout the nation now emulate, had 11 players earn all-LA City honors during an era when the LA City Section was one of the nation's top hotbeds for talent.

1985 Vista Panthers (13–0)

In an article about the state's greatest teams posted in 2015 on the CalHiSports.com website, both Steve Brand (former prep editor of *The San Diego Union-Tribune*) and Rick Smith (retired NFL public relations executive who runs the ParletonSports.com site) both chose San Diego High of 1955 as that section's best ever.

For greatest ever, though, it was tougher to pick that San Diego team too high since it technically had a tie in the CIF Southern Section semifinals. For San Diego's greatest, an argument could be made that it's Vista of 1985.

Choosing the Panthers with that accolade also is a tribute to the late Dick Haines (who won 320 games over his years at Vista and out-of-state schools) as well as to Vista quarterback Sal Aunese, who died in 1989 from a rare form of stomach cancer after helping the University of Colorado go 8–4 in 1988.

While Vista of 1985 didn't play schools from Anaheim to Los Angeles like San Diego High had to in 1955 because San Diego schools were still in the Southern Section until 1960 when their own section began, the Panthers dominated each foe and were No. 1 in the state. They won the section final 35–7 over a Helix of La Mesa team that was 11–1 and had ended the 36-game win streak of National City Sweetwater in the semifinals.

Aunese, who at one time was called "the best player I ever signed" by former Colorado assistant and former LSU head coach Les Miles, had 12 carries for 125 yards and two touchdowns in the title game. He also tossed a 60-yard scoring pass to Todd Baird.

Vista's offense also highlighted running back Roger Price, who had 1,500 yards for the season.

In a 2012 article on the team by Smith for Parleton Sports, longtime San Diego prep writer John Maffei was quoted as saying that Vista of 1985 was the best "by far" in forty years of seeing teams in the section's North County area.

1975 Cordova Lancers (11–0)

At the end of the 2014 season, the Lancers of 1975 were the ones compared the most to 16–0 Folsom as the greatest in CIF Sac-Joaquin Section history. Many in the region would rank Folsom 2014 higher, but that Folsom team was not No. 1 in the state. De La Salle of Concord was in that spot, so Folsom of 2014 has to be behind that team in the all-time comparisons. Cordova of 1975 doesn't have that problem, and besides, the Lancers of that season were an awesome group in their own right.

Cordova of '75 also represents the best team from a decade of greatness at a school that produced a 102–6–1 record, which was the best in the state and the nation.

Running head coach Dewey Guerra's wishbone offense to perfection, Cordova had little difficulty with any opponent and ended the season by rolling over Highlands (of North Highlands) 36–6 in the Capital City championship game (a precursor to the SJS playoffs that began the next season). Guerra announced soon after that game that he was leaving for American River College, but the program kept humming along for the rest of the decade under head coach Ron Lancaster.

Option quarterback Scott Jenner (who later played at Oklahoma) and fullback Max Venable (who later made it in the major leagues) led the offense, along with receiver Kenny Bowles (who later played at UNLV). The defense included future NFL player Jeff Allen in the secondary.

1978 Mt. Whitney Pioneers (13–0)

This is still the greatest team to have ever played in the CIF Central Section. Longtime section historian Bob Barnett agreed as of 2017. In addition to setting the Northern California scoring record at the time, it's a group that included three future NFL players.

Offensive lineman Don Mosebar was so dominating up front that he was named Northern California Player of the Year. He was 6-foot-7, 275 pounds and is often referred to as the best offensive lineman many longtime prep writers in the area have ever seen. One who's covered teams across the state for more than 35 years still has Mosebar No. 1. He later went on to play at USC and for many years with the Los Angeles Raiders.

The other two NFL players were senior running back Lupe Sanchez and junior receiver Mike Young. Sanchez rushed for more than 1,200 yards and scored 21 TDs for the Pioneers. He was a standout on defense and later played in the NFL as a defensive back for the Pittsburgh Steelers. Young had 13 touchdown catches and more than 1,200 receiving yards. He later played at UCLA and was in the 1989 Super Bowl with the Denver Broncos.

The Pioneers had a college-bound quarterback in senior Mark McKay as well. He didn't play in the NFL, but did start at San Diego State. McKay completed 65 percent of his passes for more than 2,000 yards and had 27 TD passes.

1916 San Diego Hilltoppers (12–0)

There just had to be one of these real old-timer teams in this book, and the Hilltoppers of 1916 surely make the grade.

Although this team was not in the 1916 CIF state playoffs, San Diego High had a 62–0 win over Long Beach Poly and only some mild difficulty with Manual Arts. The Hilltoppers also beat the USC frosh 10–7.

What sets this team apart is that the head coach, Nibs Price, later went on to have a legendary coaching career at Cal. In fact, Price was an assistant coach for the Golden Bears' 1920 national title team, dubbed the Wonder Team, that beat Ohio State in the Rose Bowl 28–0 and outscored foes 510–14.

But Price, of course, was not the only connection that this San Diego High team had to one of the most dominating college teams ever. Cal's best player, Harold "Brick" Muller—later voted the greatest player in college football between 1900 and 1925—played on that Hilltopper squad, too. College Hall of Fame lineman Stan Barnes and running back Pesky Sprott were on the same San Diego High team before going to Cal. In that Rose Bowl win, Muller played quarterback while Sprott rushed for 90 yards on 20 carries.

Bakersfield was declared the CIF state championship team for 1916 by a CIF executive committee vote and did not win on the field. San Diego High was the Southern California champion and by all indications decided not to play the Drillers. The first actual CIF state championship on the field didn't happen until 1919.

Bakersfield fans and principal A. J. Ludden were not happy. According to one newspaper report, Ludden got into his car "in a dander" and headed off to a CIF Federated Council meeting where he made an appeal that the Drillers should be declared the state champions. His argument was successful.

With all of the players that San Diego High had and what they did later on, maybe it was a good thing for Bakersfield that a game wasn't played.

4

Salute to Service

There are many players through the years who have been fiercely competitive and focused at a razor-sharp level. And then there was Pat Tillman from Leland High of San Jose in 1993.

In recruiting terms still used today, he'd be called a tweener— too small to be a linebacker and not fast enough to be a defensive back. But the way he played the game—with intelligence and great instincts to go with that intensity—created interest from some colleges and he signed a letter of intent with Arizona State.

For anyone who remembers seeing Tillman play, he's a blueprint for that type of player, one whose competitiveness and immense internal engine simply stands out on every play.

After helping Leland win a CIF Central Coast Section title in 1993, Tillman headed to Tempe and his story after that is wellknown. He became an All-American strong safety for the Sun Devils and entered the NFL with the Arizona Cardinals in 1998. As his pro career was beginning to blossom in 2002, Tillman gave it all up to join the US Army Rangers, and then in April of 2004 he was killed in Afghanistan in what later was deemed a friendly fire incident. He was twenty-seven years old.

As of early 2018, Leland High plays at Tillman Stadium and in September of 2017 a 400-pound bronze statue of Tillman was unveiled at Sun Devil Stadium in Tempe.

That kind of praise for Tillman's sacrifice is deserved, but he's far from alone. There have no doubt been hundreds if not thousands of former football players from California high schools over the years who have given their lives serving their country.

In the early 1960s, La Habra High in Orange County had an outstanding two-way player, Steve Joyner, who later became a promising defensive end at San Diego State after playing for two years at Fullerton Junior College. According to an article in *The San Diego Union-Tribune* in 2017 about a book *Promise Lost: Stephen Joyner, the Marine Corps and the Vietnam War*, Joyner gave up his SDSU career in 1966 to join the Marines. Then in 1968, while defending a hill near Khe Sahn in Vietnam, he was shot and killed. One of Joyner's coaches at San Diego State was defensive coordinator John Madden, the former Super Bowl-winning head coach of the Oakland Raiders and legendary NFL commentator.

In the Afghanistan War that began shortly after September 11, 2001, it was reported in a 2010 *Los Angeles Times* article that Buchanan High of Clovis had more former students killed as soldiers in that war (seven) than any other high school in the state.

Two of those soldiers played football for the Bears' 2000 team, which won the CIF Central Section Division I title. Jared Hubbard, twenty-two, died in action in 2004 from a roadside bomb while Nick Eishen, twenty-four, perished on Christmas Eve in 2007.

The Hubbard family also lost another son and a brother of Jared's when Nathan Hubbard perished in a helicopter crash earlier in 2007.

When the family of Nick Eishen couldn't find his football championship ring for his burial, former Buchanan coach Mike Vogt gave them his ring and Nick was buried with it.

Who Wouldn't Jump for Jack?

The other life stories among those who played high school football and then joined the military are about those who returned. Some of them who went to World War II benefitted from the GI Bill and became influential teachers and coaches.

Perhaps one of the best examples of someone who did that is Jack Ferrill, who at age ninety-one during the 2016–17 school year was still teaching physical education two days per week at a high school in Brentwood, which is in Contra Costa County. And he began teaching and coaching in 1951.

As a player, Ferrill recalls playing as an offensive lineman for the Stockton High Tarzans. Their unique nickname was derived from the Edgar Rice Burroughs book. No other high school in California before or since has used it, either. The only reason the

Tarzans don't exist today is that Stockton High itself closed in 1957.

From the late 1930s and into the early 1940s, the Tarzans were among the best in the state, and Ferrill even played for the 1943 undefeated team. He was also a coach for more than 50 years.

"I went there from 1941 to 1944 and those were great years," Ferrill said in an interview. "I was actually a swimmer and a football player and enjoyed both tremendously."

The Tarzans had an undefeated and untied team in 1938 at 9–0 that is still listed in the Cal-Hi Sports Record Book as State Team of the Year. When Jack played for the 1943 undefeated team, there weren't that many schools in the state during the war years that played too many games. Nevertheless, the undefeated status remained a bright spot. That team, coached by Larry Siemering, won three of its first four games by shutout, then topped Sacramento High 39–6. The final win was 34–19 over Grant of Sacramento.

"That was a team that just would not be beaten," he said with the same bravado that many kids have today when talking to the media. "We never were really in trouble in any of our games."

After he graduated, Ferrill joined the Marine Corps. The war was close to concluding, but he wanted to help in any way possible.

"No doubt that playing football helps in the military," Jack stated. "It's because you've already had some discipline. The first thing that happens is there's a sergeant in your face at boot camp with his finger in your face. I was able to take that I think because of football."

Ferrill didn't serve in a combat unit but was in an infantry unit and eventually settled into a role of being an orderly for superior officers. He went to Japan and served in various roles for the US occupying forces.

"Actually, you wouldn't believe how nice the Japanese people were to us in those days," he said. "Their cities and everything else was just blown apart and they were very courteous. I think maybe they were still afraid. But it was kind of amazing."

After being discharged, Ferrill went to Stockton Junior College and then used benefits of the GI Bill to get degrees from the University of the Pacific. Jack says he didn't pay one penny to go to college.

"That's the greatest thing since sliced bread," he declared of the GI Bill. "It was just a beautiful thing the government did for all of those soldiers. It made up for the time lost for all of us and it got us a lot of good leaders."

Coaching became of interest to Ferrill when he was still in college. A local high school, St. Mary's of Stockton, was struggling and needed some help. Jack helped. In the last game of that season, the Rams tied Edison of Stockton and Ferrill was hooked.

After graduating from college, Ferrill used other connections from Pacific to land a job as a physical education teacher and assistant football coach at Liberty High in Brentwood, which is a 30-minute drive west of Stockton.

For the next 13 years, Jack assisted Liberty varsity head coach Lou Bronzan. Ferrill was there in 1956 when the Lions featured one of the best players in Northern California, a versatile running back who also kicked field goals and extra points named Herm Urenda.

Urenda was selected to the 1957 North-South Shrine All-Star Classic, which in the 1950s before pro football became popular was one of the biggest football events every summer in Southern California. The 1957 Shrine game also came on the heels of the 1956 season in Southern California when two running backs at different schools—Randy Meadows of Downey and Mickey Flynn of Anaheim—seemed to capture everyone's attention.

With Meadows and Flynn both on the same team from the South, the expected large crowd arriving to watch at the Los Angeles Memorial Coliseum was way beyond what the Shriners were expecting. Estimates are that it was 85,900. It's still the largest crowd to ever witness a California high school sporting event and it's a record that is safe to say will never be broken.

Jack Ferrill was one of those who was there that night. His main objective was simply to see how one of the players he had coached at Liberty might look in an all-star game like that. Urenda not only looked good, but he was the MVP after he led the North to a stunning 32–0 victory. Urenda had 101 yards rushing, scored two touchdowns, and did the kicking for the North team.

"I was thrilled to death," Ferrill responded when asked what he thought of that night. "I got to meet a lot of the kids, too. Herman scored all those points. Here was this kid from the little town of Brentwood who stole the show.

"It was strange in a way to be in a crowd like that. But some of the people around us started cheering for Herman when they found out who we were."

Ferrill became the head coach at Liberty in 1963 and he remains that school's winningest coach in its history. In 1965, the Lions were unbeaten and had a team that is still regarded as perhaps the best in more than 100 years of the school's existence. Ferrill's team in 1969 also went unbeaten.

By 1973, Ferrill's career took a turn to the administrative side. He served in roles such as physical education chair, athletic director, vice principal, and principal until he retired in 1990.

That retirement, however, only lasted approximately two weeks until the opportunity to help out at Independence, a

Jack Ferrill holds up photo of team he coached in the 1960s at Liberty High of Brentwood. *(Mark Tennis)*

continuation high school in the same district at Liberty, became available.

In addition to teaching at Independence, Ferrill also has been serving as president of the Stockton Athletic Hall of Fame and the Liberty Joint Union High School District Hall of Fame.

"A high percentage of the kids I coached played later at state universities," Ferrill said. "I was proud of them because they never gave up. What more can a coach ask for?"

Ferrill still goes back to his military roots when thinking about many of his former players and students.

"There were two wounded in World War II from our 1943 team," he remembered. "We also had one kid [at Liberty] who was killed in Vietnam. He was a door gunner on a helicopter that crashed."

During the 2016 football season, Ferrill saw Freedom High of Oakley play several times during its 10–0 regular season and in the CIF Northern California Division 1-AA regional championship. He also reveled in Liberty winning the 2017 CIF North Coast Section Division I crown, the school's first-ever section title.

"I'm always proud of kids from the district and love to be cheering them on," he said. "I got a call just yesterday from someone who was commenting how much I influenced him as a teacher. That's what it's all about."

5

A History of the State on Index Cards

For some researchers—and one writer in particular—enthusiasm during the 2017 CIF state football playoffs was muted.

On the same week when most teams in the state were playing in the semifinal round of the CIF section playoffs, reports revealed that Bruce McIntosh, one of the earliest pioneers of high school sports research in California, was gravely ill in a Vacaville hospital.

Later on a Friday at 11:25 a.m., Bruce died at age eighty-seven from complications of that illness. He had been living in Rio Vista for the past seven years and went to the hospital in Vacaville two nights earlier. He wasn't in good health physically for several years, but he always displayed a passion for high school sports, high school football, and Notre Dame. He remained engaging and interesting to talk to right until his final day.

In the last few years of his life, Bruce became close to several neighbors in Rio Vista, including next-door neighbor Melisa Pennington and his neighbor across the court, Candy Dotson. In a phone call after Bruce's passing, Melisa said that Bruce had become "like family." Melisa, along with Candy and Melisa's sister, Priscilla Zaro, were all with Bruce at the end. For those who knew Bruce, it was good to hear that he wasn't by himself in those moments.

Bruce only lived a few blocks from Rio Vista High. He was genuinely happy to know that the Rams had won the CIF Sac-Joaquin Section Division VII title and were playing a home game in the CIF state bowl games.

The last football game that Bruce attended was a memorable one. It was at Vacaville in 2012 and the Bulldogs were playing Marin Catholic of Kentfield in a non-league game. It was a back-and-forth contest that Vacaville won 28–24. Marin Catholic, however, went on to have a better season. The Wildcats went to the CIF Division III state final before they lost to Madison of San Diego.

After that game, Bruce was excited to talk about the Marin Catholic quarterback. That's why Jeff Tedford, the head coach at Cal at the time, also was at that game. That QB was Jared Goff, who later went to Cal and became a first-round draft pick of the

Los Angeles Rams. Unfortunately for Tedford, he didn't get to develop Goff. Sonny Dykes was hired as Cal's new head coach a few weeks after that season.

The strongest connections for Bruce, though, were not for schools in Northern California. He kept detailed binders with results in all sports going back to the early 20th century of many schools in the CIF Los Angeles City Section. Bruce was from a CIF Southern Section school, South Pasadena, and before that grew up a few blocks from Long Beach Poly. Sportswriters and researchers are never supposed to have favorites, but for Bruce he definitely did and it was the Jackrabbits.

Born in Hawaii, McIntosh began keeping stats on local high school games after he moved to Long Beach and began following the Jackrabbits. High school recordkeeping remained a hobby while he was working in construction for many years in the Gardena area. He made enough of a name for himself that he became friends with Los Angeles sports icon Bill Schroeder (Helms Sports Foundation) and became pen pals with other sports researchers around the nation, including Nelson Tennis, the founder of Cal-Hi Sports.

In the 1970s, Bruce and Nelson would trade detailed letters often. Each would help with whatever project the other was working on. For Nelson, it was usually information for a California state record book he had begun, while for Bruce it was usually football scores for a collection he was building that eventually included every high school in California, some schools outside California, and even many junior colleges.

When Cal-Hi Sports initially began as a statewide newsletter in the early 1980s, Bruce was the first correspondent used for the LA City Section and for the Southern Section outside of Orange County.

Later in the 1980s, McIntosh was one of the curators for the Helms Athletic Foundation. On one visit before the opening of a museum and before all of the items were put behind glass, Bruce let a sportswriter friend of his try on a glove once worn by baseball immortal Ty Cobb and swing a bat once used by another baseball immortal, Mickey Mantle.

In the 1990s, Bruce and Nelson developed a close friendship with Fresno sports historian Bob Barnett. There was an annual trip Nelson navigated from Sacramento to Fresno (Nelson didn't drive) and then Bob drove down to San Pedro, where Bruce lived from the late 1980s until his move to Rio Vista. Those three would spend three to four days at Bruce's place, just poring over high school stats for all of their various projects. Bruce also occasionally came up to Fresno when he was still driving to meet with Nelson and Bob.

"The big three," Barnett reminisced on the day Bruce died. "I have a picture of us I look at every day. I still miss Nelson. I'm now the only one left, but great memories."

In later years, Bruce worked on a project for the CalHiSports. com website to provide interested schools around the state with detailed records and football score archives. The program wasn't free, but approximately 35 schools in 2015, 2016, and even a few in 2017 signed up.

Those football scores came from a detailed collection of index cards on which Bruce typed the result of every high school football team in California from 1892 to 2007. He donated some of those cards to the CIF Southern Section and served as a member of the CIF Southern Section selection committee that chose its 100 Athletes for 100 years.

It has been calculated that the index card collection numbers more than 300,000. That's a lot of ribbon, paper, and sore fingers.

Because of that work, on October 18, 2017, Bruce was one of six individuals honored with a Distinguished Service Award at the annual CIF Southern Section Hall of Fame inductions in Long Beach. He wasn't able to attend but was happy to receive a CIFSS Lifetime Pass. Dr. John Dahlem, who serves as a historian for the CIFSS office, was a longtime friend.

6

Gridiron Girls: Not Cute Anymore

It's no longer a human interest story about girls playing on varsity football teams. Girls are making tackles, contributing on special teams, and playing offensive positions. Many are kickers, and there's even one who is now in the state record book.

Emma Baker, who kicked for Rancho Christian of Temecula from 2014 through her senior season in 2017, doesn't look at herself as a pioneer. She's just someone doing her job. But there have been a few other females who have contributed to California prep football history as well.

During World War II, it is believed that several schools had women who served as football coaches. One known for sure took place when a woman reported as Pauline Foster guided the Corning High team as head coach in 1942. The Cardinals that year posted a 14–0 win over Orland and a 34–0 loss to Willows.

The first girl reportedly to play football in the state was Toni Ihler, who was described in a newspaper article as a "lineman" for the Portola High junior varsity in 1973. That's a small school located in the northeast Sierra Nevada Mountains.

Eleven years later, in 1984, Bridgette Farris became the first girl to score a point in a varsity game when she kicked a conversion for Hoover of Fresno in a 9–0 victory over Dinuba.

It's still unknown which girl kicked the first field goal, but the first reported "prolific" scorer was Mia Labovitz of San Diego High in 1988. That season, Labovitz made 3-of-5 field goal attempts and 5-of-7 on conversion kicks. One of those field goals was a 40-yarder in the first quarter of a game against St. Augustine of San Diego that San Diego High ended up winning 3–0. The year before, in Mia's junior season, she had a 32-yard field goal and made 8-of-9 conversions.

In 2002, Granada Hills senior Jackie Kecskes surpassed Labovitz's point totals. She made four field goals that season and had 33 PATs for a total of 45 kicking points.

In 2003, Bakersfield's Elissa White made news when she made two PATs in the first half of a 47–20 win over Foothill of Bakersfield, and then was crowned homecoming queen at halftime. There have been other female football players named homecoming queen since then, but Elissa was likely the first homecoming queen wearing a football jersey with shoulder pads on and with a crown on her head.

In 2004, Heidi Garrett from M. L. King of Riverside set a national record with a 48-yard field goal (longest ever by a girl) in her team's 24–14 victory over Paloma Valley of Menifee. She ended that season with 24 PATs and three field goals for 33 kicking points.

Girls also have done more than just score as a kicker. The first time a girl scored a touchdown in a California high school game was in 1995 when Lorenza Coronado from Jordan High of Long Beach caught a two-yard touchdown pass for the Panthers in a 34–14 win over St. Bernard of Playa del Rey. The second TD by a girl came in 2003 when Kiashira Ruiz of Gustine plunged into the end zone on a four-yard run in the closing minutes of her team's 57–28 win over Brookside Christian of Stockton.

State Champion in State Record Book

All of those girls who played before Emma Baker started playing at Rancho Christian may not have felt it at the time, but they were paving the way for others who had the same goals.

"I have talked to quite a few of them who've played before and Heidi [Garrett] is someone I've become pretty close to now," Baker said during a May 2017 interview. "We've talked about going through my journey, having to deal with boys, and a whole bunch of things. All of them have supported me through it all."

Baker's own journey began when she was in the eighth grade. That also was at Rancho Christian, since the school accepts students from kindergarten through 12th grade. The middle school football team needed a kicker. Emma had been playing club soccer since she was three years old and her father and brother thought she had the skills to do the job.

"I thought, *There's no way. That's way out of my comfort zone*," she recalled. "But eventually I decided to do it and the first time I kicked I made a field goal from about 30 to 35 yards out. It was so new, but it came naturally and I have ended up loving it."

Rancho Christian as a school was still very new at the time to having a varsity football team. The first season was in 2011, and then in early 2014, just before Baker was coming in as a freshman, a new head coach was hired. It was like striking gold. Jim Kunau came in with experience coaching at the highest levels. His 2009 team at Lutheran High in Orange County even won a CIF state title in Division II and almost was State Team of the Year.

With the backing of Kunau, Baker kept right on kicking the following season in 2014. Even though she was just a freshman, Emma was the varsity kicker and went 42-of-45 on PATs and converted three field goals.

Baker wasn't just kicking for the football team during the fall seasons, either. She was playing on the Eagles' varsity volleyball team at the same time. She'd often go back and forth from the field to the gym during practices for both teams.

It helped Emma maintain this schedule in that she was from a small school and had known some of her classmates since they were all in kindergarten. They knew what she was trying to do. She continued to kick as a sophomore and junior and continued to play volleyball.

During Baker's junior season, Rancho Christian put all the pieces together for a run at CIF Southern Section and CIF state championships. The Eagles won their section title with a 52–14 romp past Santa Ana. They then won the Division 6-AA state crown with a 38–13 triumph over Amador of Sutter Creek.

And with her team playing 16 games and finishing 14–2, Baker took advantage. Her 99 kicking points demolished the

Emma Baker gets congratulated by teammates during 2016 CIF Division 6-AA state championship game. Her team from Rancho Christian defeated Amador of Sutter Creek. *(Courtesy Baker Family)*

state record for girls kicking points and has been reported as a national record. She only missed three PATs all year out of 78 tried and went 8-for-10 on field goals with a longest of 40 yards.

In the CIF state final, Baker's one field goal and five PATs also enabled her to become the first girl to score a point in a state championship game.

"It was amazing to be part of it," Baker reflected. "To go to the practices every day to see how bad the boys wanted it was incredible."

Baker's name that season also began to be noticed not just among girl kickers. Her 99 points for a season put her into the all-time state record book and she was named to the CIF All-Southern Section Division 12 team. She became the first girl to get a listing in the state football record book along with the boys and she became the first girl ever to be named to an All-CIF Southern Section team.

Rancho Christian was moved up a division for Baker's senior season and the team's schedule was much more difficult. Still, she kept on swinging that leg and ended with 77 kicking points for a team that finished 7–5. Her final career totals of 216 PATs, 23 field goals, and 285 kicking points weren't state records, but she finished in the top five for kicking points in state history.

With those kinds of numbers, it's no wonder that Kunau and the players began to refer to Emma as "Money."

Among Baker's honors at the end of the 2017 season was being selected second team all-state small schools kicker. She became the first girl to be on any all-state team since the teams began to be compiled within California in 1980.

"Emma's consistency over these years has been off the charts," Kunau told the Riverside *Press-Enterprise* in 2016. "She's that reliable. She is unflappable out on the field."

"A lot of people put it on me when I kick a field goal," Baker stated. "But I wouldn't be where I am today without my teammates. They're the reason I kick and the reason I've scored so many points."

Emma's teammates didn't just give her moral support. There were times when they physically had to protect her from opponents looking to take out a girl with a bone-crunching hit.

"Yes, there have been guys trying to hit me," she said. "They don't think I belonged in the sport. It was kind of a message like 'Don't come on my field.' But the guys on my line just weren't going to let that happen. I have been in a few situations where I could have gotten hit, but I was not scared."

The most pressure that Baker faced while kicking for the Eagles, however, wasn't so much on the field.

"It's probably all the stuff that gets online. Some of my kicks had a million page views. It can feel like all the pressure is on me. But mentally I can't let anything bother me. It's just about that one kick at that one moment."

And freezing those moments in time are what high school football is all about.

7

Breaking State Records

Some state football records are broken with surprisingly little fanfare. Perhaps because the achievement is expected or sometimes because the record in question isn't from one of the most prestigious categories, some players and coaches involved just don't see the moment as one to be cherished.

But there are other record-breaking achievements in which

the players, their families, and school communities fully embrace everything surrounding it.

One of the most personally memorable such achievements took place in mid-November of 1989 at Poly High in Sun Valley. It was a regular season final game for the team at Franklin High of Los Angeles and Franklin quarterback Santiago Alvarez had a chance to become the state's all-time single-season leader for touchdown passes.

Alvarez began the night with 40 TD passes in nine games and needed four to tie the state record at the time of 44 set in the previous season (1988) by Jim McKinley from Menlo School of Atherton. He had four in the fourth quarter, and even though the Franklin team was leading Eagle Rock 35–0 head coach Armando Gonzalez instructed the senior quarterback to go for the record. Alvarez got it on a 52-yard pass to Adrian Wong.

After the game, dozens of Alvarez's family and friends surrounded him. It appeared as if one or two grandmas were in tears. At least two older men (perhaps an uncle or two) had big smiles on their faces after they had obviously attended the game after work, their pants splattered in oil and grease. Seeing Alvarez break a California high school record was not just going to be a great memory for the player involved but for the entire Alvarez family.

"This is the greatest feeling I've had since I began playing football," said Alvarez, who ended the game with 337 yards passing and five touchdowns. "I have to give all the credit to my coaches and offensive line."

Fast forward a few years, and Alvarez's state record (he would end the season with 52 touchdown passes) has been eclipsed many times. Today, it doesn't even seem that high. Still, in that moment in 1989, no quarterback in California history had as many touchdown passes in one season, and for that family that was a moment they will always have etched in their memories.

Tulare's Terror

A similar Cal-Hi Sports trip as to the one in 1989 to the San Fernando Valley was planned in November of 2017 from Stockton to Tulare to watch senior running back Kazmeir Allen of Tulare High break the state record for most touchdowns scored in one season. Allen had been on a tear and only needed one touchdown to tie and two to break the state record of 64 that was set in 2000 by Tyler Ebell of Ventura.

Although the trip was cut short by a non-injury car accident, Allen didn't disappoint on that night. He rushed for 191 yards on 22 carries and scored three times to lead Tulare to a 42–12 victory over Garces of Bakersfield in the CIF Central Section Division II semifinals.

Allen wasn't done after that night, either. In the Tribe's first CIF Central Section Division II playoff game against Sunnyside of Fresno, he broke loose for 434 yards rushing on 31 carries and scored eight touchdowns. That gave Allen the chance to break the national single-season record. Even though Tulare couldn't get past Serra of San Mateo in the CIF Division 2-AA Northern California regional final, Allen didn't let that stop him from making history.

In that regional final, Allen continued to surge with 27 carries for 347 yards and two scores, plus he took a kickoff return and brought it back for a 96-yard touchdown. Despite all that, Serra's offense proved to be even more unstoppable as the Padres ended Allen's season with a wild-and-wacky 76–43 win. The next week after Serra won the state title, its head coach, Patrick Walsh, who has been around California football since he was a running back himself at De La Salle (Concord) in the early 1990s, called Allen "the best running back I've ever seen."

Tulare head coach Darren Bennett, who has been coaching there since 1995, also heaped a lot of praise on Allen for the 2017 season he had.

"He was just so explosive," Bennett said. "We had a lot of one-play drives for touchdowns because of him and I've never seen anybody ever with so many one-play touchdowns. He's the best I've seen."

After the Serra game, Allen finished with 72 touchdowns scored. He established a new national record, surpassing the previous all-time best mark of 71 set in 2001 by T. A. McLendon of Albemarle, NC. He also led the state with 3,336 yards rushing.

"Before the season when I had committed to Boise State, the coach who was recruiting me told me the national record was 71 and that he needed me to break it," Allen recalled. "I didn't think that was possible, but then when I was in the 50s and still had a lot more games left I thought it could happen."

Allen benefited from a record-breaking angle by several other factors. First, while Tulare's offense with himself, junior quarterback Nathan Lamb, and senior wide receiver Emoryie Edwards was virtually unstoppable, the defense wasn't very strong. This prevented the team from being ahead by such a large margin so that the starting players had to continue to play and continue to score. Second, Edwards suffered injuries that limited his production, which enticed Bennett to go to Allen and the running game a lot more often.

"It was kind of a perfect storm," remembered Bennett, who ended the 2017 season needing just three more wins to reach 200 for his coaching career. "Emoryie got hurt and that did really open the door for Kazmeir."

Allen has always been super-fast, which was shown during the spring of his junior year when he went out for the Tulare track team for the first time. Despite just two months of training, he went all the way to the CIF state final in the 100-meter dash. Allen picked up a medal with a sixth-place finish, but his time of 10.48 seconds would have won titles in more than half of the states in the nation.

When he was a sophomore, Allen only weighed about 140 pounds, Bennett says. Allen wasn't expecting to play much on the varsity football team, but senior Romello Harris missed some games with injuries and Allen had to step up. Allen had one outing that season with 36 carries for 330 yards and three touchdowns and 18 carries for 321 yards and four scores.

"A lot of what's happened to me is from him," Allen said of Harris, who finished his career at Tulare in 2015 with 7,311 career rushing yards and 91 career touchdowns and who was preparing to play in 2018 for Fresno State. "He taught me all of the plays. I learned a lot from him and looked up to him."

Tulare also has been a school with one of the greatest running back traditions of any school in California. In 1947, the star running back was senior Bob Mathias, who less than one year later was the gold medal winner in the decathlon at the Olympic Games in London. And in addition to Allen and Harris, there was running back Dominique Dorsey at Tulare from 1998–2000. He set the state career rushing record at 7,761 yards in 2000 (it was broken the next season) and is still among the all-time state leaders with 118 career touchdowns.

"Kazmeir has worked so hard in the classroom and in the weight room and deserves what he's getting," Bennett said. "He built himself up to 182 pounds as a senior, but it didn't hurt his speed. Now, he has a chance to be one of the best ever from California."

Allen wasn't in any of the All-American all-star games because those rosters are basically set more than a year in advance and don't have a process for making changes based on what happens during a player's senior season. College coaches, though, began to heat up on Allen during the season. Despite Allen's commitment to Boise State, Wisconsin came in with an offer and then when UCLA hired former NFL head coach and former Oregon head coach Chip Kelly, one of the first things Kelly did was take a trip to Tulare. He offered Allen, and the switch from Boise State to the Bruins was made.

"It's great that all of these records and everything has been recorded," Allen said. "If I tell someone I scored 72 touchdowns, it's easy to show that I'm not making stuff up. The whole thing was a good experience. Maybe I might get to show my son someday."

Folsom's Phenom

As far as debut performances go, the one by Jake Browning as a first-time sophomore starting quarterback at Folsom in August of 2012 was about as good as it gets.

Browning was being elevated to the varsity starting job after starring on Folsom's freshman team the year before. His father, Ed, was a star quarterback at La Sierra High in Riverside in the 1980s and later played at Oregon State, but not much beyond the Folsom locker room was known about the team's new starter.

The identity of the next quarterback at Folsom in 2012 actually was one of the biggest questions in Northern California prep football prior to the season. The team's 2011 starter, senior Tanner Trosin, had set the state single-season record with 5,185 yards. The starter for 2009 and 2010, Dano Graves, had passed for 62 touchdowns in 2010 and had led the Bulldogs to their first

CIF state title (which came in Division II and was against a Serra of Gardena team that included future NFL stars Adoree' Jackson and Marqise Lee).

It turned out that Trosin and Graves were just warm-up acts for Browning. In his very first game on an August night against Woodcreek of Roseville, the sophomore debuted with 34 completions in 51 attempts for a Northern California record 689 yards. He also had 10 touchdown passes, which tied the state record of 10 set in 1999 by David Koral from Palisades of Pacific Palisades.

"I don't think anyone knew what we could do before that season, but I knew and that team we were playing kept blitzing so there were a lot of bubbles [screen passes] that were always there that went for scores," Browning said during a 2017 interview at Pac-12 media day. "It didn't take long for me to get interviews. I'd never been interviewed before and the next week ESPN and *USA Today* were calling. I just didn't want to say anything stupid."

Browning finished that sophomore season with 5,248 yards in 15 games and broke the state record that Trosin had set the year before. He also surpassed Dano Graves's school record for touchdown passes with 63, which tied the state record of 63 that was set in 1999 by Robert De La Cruz from Cathedral of Los Angeles.

As a junior, Browning improved in all facets of his game, particularly running for first downs. He not only broke the state yardage record once again but completely shattered it with 5,704 yards. He also ended with 75 touchdown passes to obliterate his own co-record.

The only downer for those first two seasons for Browning is that the Folsom team had to go up against national powerhouse De La Salle of Concord in the CIF Northern California Open

Division championship. It was a step up in competition that the Bulldogs weren't quite ready for. They lost both games, 49–15 and 45–17.

With most of the team coming back in 2014, including Browning, the Bulldogs were forecast to be much better. There were other players coming into the lineup as well, especially junior offensive tackle Jonah Williams.

The Bulldogs opened the 2016 season in San Diego and topped Cathedral Catholic 55–10 in a showing that was so impressive that longtime Cathedral Catholic head coach Sean Doyle called them "the best team I've ever seen." They pummeled perennial powers like Granite Bay (63–0) and Del Oro of Loomis (42–7) and went on to win their third straight CIF Sac-Joaquin Section title with a 55–7 romp past Tracy.

There was a change in the CIF regional playoffs, however, that eliminated the Northern California Open Division game in 2014 and automatically sent teams selected for the NorCal and Southern California Open Divisions directly into the state finals. Due to De La Salle's wins over Folsom the previous two seasons, the Spartans were chosen for that game. The Bulldogs instead were placed into the Northern California Division I final, which still turned out to be a huge game locally because opponent Grant of Sacramento also was 14–0.

Grant and Folsom had previously staged two huge showdowns in the 2010 season, with Grant winning the first time before a national television audience on ESPN and Folsom winning in the section final. In 2014, Grant had no chance. Browning only threw for 292 yards and three touchdowns, but the Bulldogs rolled 52–21.

That win sent Folsom to the CIF Division I state championship at the StubHub Center in Carson, where the team would face Oceanside. Even though Oceanside scored first, it was a showcase for Browning and the Bulldogs. They won 68–7 in the most lopsided CIF state final ever. Browning completed 27 of 35 passes for 439 yards and six scores.

In addition to winding up a 16–0 season, Folsom had scored 915 points to become the highest-scoring team in state and US history. There's no question it was one of the best teams in California history, but questions about whether it's *the* best will always remain because the Bulldogs were not in the Open Division; they didn't get to play De La Salle; and they never played a Southern California Open Division squad like Centennial of Corona, St. John Bosco, or Mater Dei. De La Salle, by the way, won the CIF Open Division title that season with a win over Centennial and like Folsom also was unbeaten.

"I wouldn't say I regret we didn't get to play them, but it would have been cool to play them," Browning commented. "It still was pretty special. Our whole senior class that year was just everybody playing together. Even all of the years leading up to that were special. I remember getting hit so hard when I was eight years old by Eddie Flores that I cried. Eddie and I and so many others all grew up together. For the whole program at Folsom, it was just a lot of guys who grew up together."

It wasn't certain that Browning would break his own state single-season yardage record as a senior because the Bulldogs took their foot off the gas in the second half of many games, but the extra game enabled him to get to 5,790 yards. There was no doubt about touchdown passes. Browning had one game with eight TDs and three more with seven. His final total of 91 TDs was a new national record. He also set a national record with 229 career TD passes and finished with 16,775 career passing yards. That wasn't a national record, but may be a state record for a long, long time.

If there has been one player in the last two decades who has made the editors of Cal-Hi Sports work the hardest on updating state records, it has been Folsom's Jake Browning. He played for the Bulldogs from 2012 to 2014. *(James K. Leash/SportStars)*

"Looking back at all the records and all the titles it was just special," Browning said. "Folsom is still kind of a small place and they're still doing well. All the hard work we put into it made it pretty special."

Browning did most of that work with Folsom's co-head coach at the time, Troy Taylor, who left the school after the 2015 season to become offensive coordinator at Eastern Washington. Taylor, a former quarterback at Cal and an all-state quarterback in the 1990s at Cordova of Rancho Cordova, then left Eastern Washington after one season to become offensive coordinator at the University of Utah for the 2017 season.

Kris Richardson was the head coach at Folsom before Taylor assumed a co-coaching role in 2011, and Richardson continued in that role after Taylor left. In the 2017 season, Folsom went 16–0, winning its third CIF state title, and Richardson was named Cal-Hi Sports State Coach of the Year.

Browning was ready to move on to the University of Washington after that last game in Carson and less than two weeks later already was attending classes in Seattle. He won the starting job for the Huskies as a true freshman for the 2015 season, then in 2016 he was Offensive Player of the Year in the Pac-12 Conference. Browning suffered a shoulder injury that required surgery after 2016, however, and didn't have as strong of a season in 2017.

"The best part about coming from Folsom is that in college I was just expecting to throw a touchdown pass every time we got the ball," Browning said. "We had such high expectations and with Coach Taylor it was run like a college program. I actually spent more time in high school doing football stuff every week than I do now because of the 20-hour rule. Just by Thursday at Folsom I had spent more time in a week working on a game plan as I can do now."

What Browning and his teammates at Folsom probably don't know is how much time it took to rewrite all of those state record lists.

Centennial's Inspiration

If Folsom or a player from Folsom isn't breaking a state record during a California football season, then there's a good chance that the record-breaking is coming from Centennial High of Corona.

While Folsom is the only team in state history to score 900 points or more in a season, the Centennial Huskies are the only offense to pile up more than 9,000 total yards. They did that in the 2013 season, in just 15 games (compared to 16 by many teams that have set records since the 2006 season). Centennial also is the only school in California history to have two 800-point seasons, with 800 in 2013 and 812 in 2015. The 2012 squad went way beyond 8,000 yards of total offense as well with 8,570 yards.

Centennial's offense tends to get even more yards than Folsom because in its offense the running back often will have just as many yards rushing as the quarterback does with passing.

When the program was gaining momentum in the early 2000s under head coach Matt Logan, the Huskies played in the CIF Southern Section Inland Division. They won section titles in 2000, 2002, 2004, 2007, 2008, 2010, 2012, and 2013. They were moved up to the top division of the section for 2014, which was then called the Pac-5 Division. Despite the increased level of competition, Centennial beat St. John Bosco of Bellflower (the No. 1 team in the state in 2013) in both the 2014 and 2015 championship games.

At the CIF state level, the highlight for the Huskies was outlasting 2007 state champion and nationally renowned De La Salle of Concord 21–16 for the Division I state title in 2008. With future NFL linebacker Vontaze Burfict and several others on defense who would later play in the NFL, Centennial capped a 15–0 season and was the No. 1 team in the state. The team lost to De La Salle in the 2007 state championships and then lost to the Spartans again in 2012, 2014, and 2015.

When Centennial did get that state title in 2008, it was a bittersweet moment watching Logan celebrating on the field with his three daughters and other family members. One family member who wasn't there was his wife, Donna. She had died in July of 2007 at age forty-one of breast cancer.

Donna Logan's fight to stave off breast cancer was almost epic. She was first diagnosed in May of 2003 and immediately began treatment. According to media reports, she underwent 36

If there has been one coach in the last two decades who has made the editors of Cal-Hi Sports work the hardest on updating state records, it has been Corona Centennial's Matt Logan. He celebrates 2015 CIF Southern Section Pac-5 Division title. *(Mark Tennis)*

radiation treatments in May of 2004. In February of 2005, she and Matt spent more than a month at Duke University in North Carolina, where she received a bone marrow transplant. That was followed by more radiation treatments, and then in 2006 she had lymph nodes taken out and underwent more chemotherapy. She started hospice care by February of 2007 and was gone a few months later.

Several years later, in 2012, one of Logan's daughters, Samantha, was playing in a powder puff football game and threw several passes that were both accurate and quickly delivered. Her father came up with an idea that perhaps she could play on the Centennial varsity squad and become the second girl in California history to throw a touchdown pass. Samantha did end up playing in one game, where she completed an 18-yard pass to Jordan Dye, though she didn't get that touchdown. She wore a uniform that was adorned with a pink towel as well as pink socks.

Matt Logan finished the 2017 season with 230 wins and just 49 losses in a head coaching career that began in 1997. He and his coaching staff have been able to keep their program at the elite level as a public school in an era when private schools have been bolstering their rosters with major college recruits as transfers. It's been inspiring to many others to watch, especially once they know the heartbreak of his past.

8

A Record That Should Never Fall

If there's ever a game in which a California high school football player has scored 10 touchdowns, somebody better get a message to the head coach so that he or she makes sure that player does not score an 11th.

That's because the Cal-Hi Sports state record of scoring 11 touchdowns in one game deserves to stay in the sole possession of Frank Greene, who did it during a 1929 game for Coronado High in a 108–0 victory over Sweetwater of National City.

In those days, Coronado only had a school enrollment of just over 300 and a roster of 18 players, so it wasn't like head coach A. E. Schaefer could have taken out Greene from a lopsided contest even if he wanted to.

Although the game against Sweetwater in which Greene scored 11 touchdowns and had 14 points on conversions for a single-game total of 80 points is the one that put him in the record books, the most memorable game for him and his Coronado teammates was the one played that season against Long Beach Poly.

Despite its low number of players, Coronado was one of the best teams in all of Southern California. With Greene and quarterback Johnny Lyons, the team won the 1929 Southern Prep League championship. There were no playoffs in those days, but Coronado's final game was against Poly, which was the champion from another league.

Even then, the Jackrabbits represented a huge student body and the enrollment differential was 3,500 for Poly to just over 300 for Coronado. It was a Hoosiers-style matchup in California football if there ever was one.

Although Coronado didn't win on some miracle last-second play, the team battled on even terms with Poly for almost the entire duration. In the first half, Greene threw a touchdown pass and kicked the extra point to give Coronado a 7–6 lead. The small team held on to that 7–6 lead midway into the fourth quarter. It wasn't until the Jackrabbits completed two long passes to set up touchdowns that they eventually crafted a 20–7 victory.

Still, Greene went on to star in college with Lyons at the University of Tulsa and is still regarded as one of the best players that Tulsa has ever had. When Greene was there, he ran and kicked his college team to victories over Oklahoma, Kansas, and Arkansas.

In the early 1930s, after Greene had finished playing in college, pro football options for those like him were very limited. Nevertheless, he gave it a try anyway and for three seasons was a member of the Chicago Cardinals. He also helped coach and worked for a team in Los Angeles that was called the Bulldogs (later became the Rams of the NFL).

After 1936, Greene began to think about heading home. He eventually became a member of the Coronado Police Department.

By 1954, when Greene was forty-three and had a wife and teenage son (who was going to Coronado High), he had risen to the rank of lieutenant and would often be the acting Chief of Police if the Chief of Police was out of town.

On October 12, 1954, Greene took the night shift and was patrolling the streets of Coronado with Richard Lutsey, a US Navy shore patrolman.

At approximately two a.m., Greene and Lutsey stopped a car with three men inside near the public library and main plaza of the town.

According to newspaper accounts at the time, Greene walked to the driver's window and looked inside. The driver exited the car and after a few moments Greene noticed a gun on the opposite floorboard. Lutsey later said a scuffle ensued and the driver, later identified as twenty-seven-year-old Robert Rodriguez, was able to pull out a different gun that he had in his waistband and shot Frank Greene in the head.

Lutsey leapt from the police car and immediately apprehended the passenger who was in the back seat, later identified as thirty-nine-year-old Benjamin Porozowski. Rodriguez and the other man, thirty-five-year-old Rafael Gruber, who was in the front seat of the shooter's car, fled on foot.

Nothing could be done for Greene. It was later reported that he probably died instantly.

What transpired after the shooting was called at the time in San Diego "the city's record manhunt." With the aid of the US Coast Guard and US Navy patrolmen, the island of Coronado was effectively sealed and eventually a massive total of 5,000 homes was searched, one by one.

By 1:15 p.m. the next day, Rodriguez was captured while hiding in an attic at a hotel. Gruber remained at-large for nearly 24 hours until he turned himself in at the US border with Mexico.

All three suspects were eventually tried and convicted of murder and reportedly received life sentences. It also was later revealed that they were workers at the famous Hotel Del Coronado who were planning to go on a robbery spree when they were stopped by Greene and Lutsey.

Greene's death would have shaken up the San Diego community regardless, but as a former local sports hero it perhaps shook it up even worse.

Wrote legendary San Diego sports columnist Jack Murphy two days after the shooting: "Frank Greene was a man who could cope with any situation. But his killer didn't give him a chance."

The next time you see Frank Greene's name mentioned whenever someone in California scores nine or 10 touchdowns in a game, remember that there's more to that name than just a line in a record book. His name also appears on the Police Officer's Memorial in Sacramento. It truly represents a state record that should last forever.

9

California Quarterbacks
Second to None

It already seemed like New England Patriots quarterback and California native Tom Brady had experienced a coronation as the greatest quarterback in NFL history before he even took the field in Super Bowl LII in Minneapolis. That came in February 2017 at the Super Bowl in Houston when Brady and the Patriots came back from a 28–3 deficit in the third quarter to stun the Atlanta

Falcons 34–28 in overtime and win for the fifth time with him as their quarterback.

A sixth Super Bowl title was not to be. Even though Brady passed for a Super Bowl record 505 yards and four touchdowns, the Patriots couldn't come back from a 10-point deficit in the second half and lost to the Philadelphia Eagles 41–33. It was the third time they had lost in a Super Bowl with Brady starting. Still, his eight appearances in the biggest game of them all is another record. No other player on that list is shown even with seven.

Before the win against the Falcons in 2017, Brady had been in a tie with Joe Montana, his boyhood idol, of the San Francisco 49ers and Terry Bradshaw of the Pittsburgh Steelers as the only quarterbacks to lead their teams to four Super Bowl crowns. Brady also was MVP of Super Bowl LI, which was his fourth and again put him ahead of any other quarterback.

Montana was Brady's idol because Brady grew up on the San Francisco Peninsula. He attended Serra High of San Mateo, a school noted for having had several other prominent athletes before him, including Super Bowl X MVP Lynn Swann (a favorite receiver of Bradshaw's) and baseball home run king Barry Bonds.

Neither Montana or Bradshaw is from a California high school, but Brady is not alone as a quarterback from the Golden State who has subsequently guided a team to the Vince Lombardi Trophy.

It took seven attempts before the first one was able to do it. That happened in 1981 when Jim Plunkett (James Lick High of San Jose) helped the Oakland Raiders top the Eagles in Super Bowl XV. The previous six who lost in the Super Bowl as starters were Craig Morton (Campbell) twice, Daryle Lamonica (Clovis), Joe Kapp (Hart of Newhall), Bill Kilmer (Citrus of Azusa), and Vince Ferragamo (Banning of Wilmington).

Plunkett won the Super Bowl for the second time two years later for the Los Angeles Raiders in Super Bowl XVII. John Elway (Granada Hills) then made three attempts to be a Super Bowl-winning quarterback in 1987, 1988, and 1990 for the Denver Broncos. He finally won one in Super Bowl XXXII in 1997 as the Broncos prevented the Green Bay Packers from repeating. The next year Elway was the one who repeated in leading Denver past Atlanta in Super Bowl XXXIII.

The third from the state to do it was Trent Dilfer (Aptos) of the Baltimore Ravens. He earned his ring when the Ravens defeated the New York Giants in Super Bowl XXXIV in 2001.

Brady came on to the scene the next season to win his very first Super Bowl, a victory against the favored St. Louis Rams. His subsequent Super Bowl titles have come in 2004, 2005, 2015, and 2017.

The only other California quarterback to guide a team to a Super Bowl win has been Aaron Rodgers of the Green Bay Packers. He is from Pleasant Valley High of Chico. The Packers knocked off the Pittsburgh Steelers in Super Bowl XLV in 2011.

Dilfer Drops Dimes

If there's ever been an NFL quarterback who can talk about the position with passion, who's been around some of the greatest coaches and players, and who has a way of connecting with young quarterbacks as a coach himself, then Trent Dilfer would be that guy.

Dilfer became the third quarterback from California to start for a winning team in the Super Bowl when the Baltimore Ravens beat up the New York Giants 34–7 at Super Bowl XXXV in January of 2001 at Raymond James Stadium in Tampa, Florida. Dilfer threw a 38-yard touchdown pass to Brandon Stokley for the first score of the game and then watched his defensive team-mates not allow the Giants to score once. New York's only TD came on a kickoff return.

Growing up in Santa Cruz County, away from the bright lights and concentrated media of Southern California or the San Francisco Bay Area, Dilfer was one of those athletes who simply loved to play sports. At Aptos High, he was just as dominant on the basketball court in the winter and for the golf team in the spring.

"A lot of my football memories from then are not quarterback-centric but team-centric," Dilfer said during a July 2017 phone interview. "We really pulled up the program at Aptos. Our class kind of pulled them from out of the ashes. It was kind of like a band of brothers playing together for a common goal.

"From a quarterback standpoint, it was just a chance to compete. I wasn't a great player, but loved having the ball in my hands with a chance to decide the game. Whether I handed it to my running back Mike Brady or whether I was throwing it to Mike Fuller my receiver or running it myself, I was the one deciding the outcome."

During his high school career at Aptos, Dilfer was all-league in football, basketball, and golf and led Mariners teams into the CIF Central Coast Section playoffs in all three sports. After the 1989–90 school year, Trent was selected as the Santa Cruz County Athlete of the Year by the *Santa Cruz Sentinel*.

While it worked out for Dilfer to play multiple sports in high school, many of the best developing young quarterbacks in the 2010s have dropped other sports. Their belief, often promoted by a private quarterback instructor, is to become as polished as possible as a quarterback as early as possible.

"I wish they would [keep playing other sports]," Dilfer declared. "I saw recently that 96 percent of NFL quarterbacks

Trent Dilfer stands in front of some of the high school quarterbacks he is going to instruct during The Opening that was held in July of 2015 at Nike World Headquarters in Oregon. *(Jake Zembiec/Student Sports)*

were dual-sport athletes in high school. I loved playing multiple sports and I know it hurt my recruiting, but it was such a great experience. I was a much better basketball player back then than football. You've just got to trust that you'll find a college coach who will mold you into the type of player you can be.

"Now, I get it while so many feel the pressure to be honing their craft, to get polished early to impress evaluators. And there are other kids who don't want to be a backup or the seventh or eighth player on a basketball team. When the choice is for another sport, no matter the role, they're going to learn so much about the role of all players for any team."

For Dilfer, the college coach who primarily molded him into an NFL draft prospect was Jeff Tedford at Fresno State. Tedford, who is from Warren High of Downey and would later be credited most often with developing Aaron Rodgers at Cal into a first-round prospect, coached Dilfer during his first years as the head coach of the Bulldogs from 1993 to 1997. Tedford returned to Fresno State in 2017 to serve another tenure as its head coach.

By the time of the 1994 NFL Draft, Dilfer had become known as one of the top quarterbacks any team could choose. He had 19 school records at Fresno State and led the nation in passing efficiency. He ended up being selected with the sixth pick in the first round by the Tampa Bay Buccaneers.

That 1994 NFL Draft also was a bonanza for California in general. The state often ranks at the top or near the top for all states in having the most high school graduates in every NFL Draft, but in 1994 there were eight from California among the first 23 chosen in the first round. And going into the second round, there were 12 from the Golden State out of the first 38 players selected. Texas that year only had four in the first round and Florida only had two.

Seven others joined Dilfer as first-rounders from California in 1994: linebacker Willie McGinest of Long Beach Poly (4th by New England); linebacker Jamir Miller of El Cerrito (10th to Arizona); offensive tackle Aaron Taylor from De La Salle of Concord (16th to Green Bay); wide receiver Charles Johnson from Cajon of San Bernardino (17th to Pittsburgh); offensive tackle Todd Steussie of Agoura (19th to Minnesota); wide receiver Johnnie Morton from South of Torrance (21st to Detroit); and defensive end Shante Carver from Lincoln of Stockton (23rd to Dallas).

Of course, first round quarterbacks in the NFL Draft from California aren't that rare. For about half of all NFL drafts ever done, there's at least one. But at the end of the 2017 college season, three from the Golden State were projected to be first-rounders in 2018—Josh Rosen from St. John Bosco of Bellflower, Sam

Darnold of San Clemente, and Josh Allen of Firebaugh. It seems surreal to put a quarterback from the tiny San Joaquin Valley town of Firebaugh up near Rosen (UCLA) and Darnold (USC), but Allen went to the University of Wyoming after a stop at Reedley College, got himself much bigger and stronger, and improved in all facets of his game. The only year prior to 2018 in which there were three first-round quarterbacks in the draft was 1983 with John Elway (Granada Hills), Tony Eason (Delta of Clarksburg), and Ken O'Brien (Jesuit of Carmichael).

With that many first-round picks, it therefore shouldn't be a surprise to anyone to learn that during one week of the 2017 season in the NFL there were nine teams that had starting quarterbacks from California high schools. That didn't include Colin Kaepernick from Pitman of Turlock, who started for the San Francisco 49ers in a Super Bowl but wasn't signed as a free agent.

Dilfer became a backup quarterback later in his career. He started for Tampa Bay for five of his first six seasons in the league and had up-and-down performances. There was one season—1996—when Dilfer helped the team get to the playoffs for the first time in 15 years. He also averaged more than 2,700 yards for the four years from 1996 to 1999. On the down side, Dilfer had four touchdown passes and 18 interceptions in his second season in 1997. The Super Bowl season then came in 2000 with the Ravens, which despite that achievement didn't land Dilfer a starting job. He was a backup to Matt Hasselbeck in Seattle for several seasons, and then in 2005 he was with the Cleveland Browns.

Dilfer's final stop was with the San Francisco 49ers. He played the 2007 season there, mainly to serve as a mentor for 49ers' No. 1 draft pick Alex Smith (who is also from California, from Helix of La Mesa). Dilfer retired after the 2008 season after suffering a concussion in a December game against the Minnesota Vikings, although he later said he was planning on retiring regardless of that injury or an Achilles heel injury he suffered playing basketball.

Any career with a Super Bowl ring has a magical tinge to it. For Dilfer, though, his years in the NFL were marked with a personal tragedy. That came in the spring of 2003 when he and his wife, Cassandra, who was a former swimmer at Fresno State, lost their five-year-old son, Trevin, to a heart condition. The growing family—he and Cassandra also have three daughters—was living in California at the time while Trent was playing for Seattle. Trevin's heart became infected with a virus. He battled it for 40 days until he died in April at Stanford University's Lucille Packard Children's Hospital.

Several years later, the foundation that Dilfer had set up to honor Trevin donated funds to help Aptos High upgrade its football stadium and athletic facilities. The school now plays its games at Trevin Dilfer Stadium.

Just after he retired from playing quarterback, Dilfer began talking about it on air for ESPN. He did a few games as a color analyst, but primarily did the cross-country trek from the Bay Area to ESPN's studios in Bristol, Connecticut, to be featured on numerous NFL shows. He became best known for "Dilfer's Dimes," a segment in which he highlighted the best throws each week by NFL quarterbacks. The phrase has become common at all levels of the game. So the next time you see a quarterback throwing a perfectly-timed, perfectly-placed pass and that pass is referred to "as a dime," that's from Dilfer.

As he was being interviewed for this book, Dilfer was in transition because he had been laid off by ESPN after a nine-year career in April of 2017 and was preparing to move from the Bay

Area to Austin, Texas. One of his daughters, Tori, already had moved to Texas and was playing volleyball at TCU. Another daughter, Maddie, was playing beach volleyball at Pepperdine while the youngest daughter, Delaney, was playing at Vandegrift High in Austin, Texas. Both Maddie and Tori were all-state volleyball players at Valley Christian High in San Jose.

Coaching became a possibility for Dilfer when, in 2010, he began working with ESPN and events company Student Sports as the head coach of the annual Elite 11 Quarterback camps and events. The Elite 11 offers a series of regional-based tryouts that are formatted more like a clinic in which top quarterbacks from throughout the nation are invited. The final 24 of those quarterbacks are then invited to the Elite 11 finals, where they are paired down to just 11 and then those 11 are invited to participate in Nike's huge summer kickoff, known as The Opening.

Perhaps because he was about to move to Texas, Dilfer wouldn't say that California is the best state for quarterbacks, but he offered a lot of praise.

"It's definitely not lacking in great players coming out at the quarterback position," he said. "In my seven years with the Elite 11, the three major hotbeds have been California, Texas, and Georgia. Every year we know we can count on guys from those states who can really throw the ball."

Reasons for California's dominance at the position range from the obvious, such as the large population and mild weather, to the not-so-obvious.

"There is a lot of good high school football and good coaches," he continued. "A lot of colleges also have a history of throwing the ball whether you're from San Diego, Orange County, or Northern California. Kids grow up here knowing they've got a chance to throw it around a bit. And you've got coaches here who have been going to clinics for years, even going back to Bill Walsh, Don Coryell, Norv Turner, and Denny Green."

Dilfer thinks that Rosen and Darnold both have a chance to be "very good" in the NFL and singled out Stanford's K. J. Costello (Santa Margarita of Rancho SM) and USC's JT Daniels (Mater Dei of Santa Ana) for having great potential as well. Both Rosen and Darnold were Elite 11 quarterbacks with Dilfer, as was 2016 No. 1 NFL Draft pick Jared Goff, who is from Marin Catholic of Kentfield and who emerged as a top-flight NFL quarterback in his second season with the Los Angeles Rams.

One of Dilfer's top concerns about quarterbacks coming up, however, is that some of them depend too much on their personal, private coach and not as much on their high school coach.

"They feel like they're the kid's coach," Dilfer lamented about many of the private quarterback coaches. "But to me they're like a swing coach in golf. I use the golf analogy all the time. The kid [as a quarterback] ultimately needs to self-correct and not use the private quarterback coach as a crutch. I'm not saying all private coaches are like that, but the best ones say, 'Here's a craft. Let's get you the skills to self-correct.' You have to empower the kid to fix himself."

More on Brady

As the future NFL legend was growing up in San Mateo County playing both football and baseball, the first person from his family to gain wide recognition in athletics was not Tom Brady himself but his older sister, Maureen. And even after Brady graduated from Serra High in 1995, he never came close to the high school athletic accomplishments of his sister.

Maureen Brady, you see, is still known as one of the most dominating high school softball pitchers in California history.

She didn't go to Serra (that's an all-boys school) but instead went to public Hillsdale High in San Mateo. Maureen began throwing no-hitters and perfect games at Hillsdale as a freshman in 1988 and continued to do so for three more years. In her junior season in 1990, Brady set Cal-Hi Sports state records with 32 wins (she was 32–1) and six perfect games. She ended her career in 1991 as the first pitcher in California history to win 100 games (she won 111 against just 10 losses) and set a state record for most perfect games in a career (14). Maureen also tied a state record held at the time by the softball legend Lisa Fernandez with 69 career shutouts.

All of Maureen Brady's state softball records have since been broken, but she remains prominent in the state record book. She later went on to pitch for Fresno State, and in 2017 her daughter, Maya, who was at Oaks Christian of Westlake Village, was one of the top softball prospects in the nation. Maya is expected to enroll as a freshman at UCLA in 2019 with a full-ride softball scholarship.

Maureen's younger brother didn't have a similar record-breaking career at Serra. Though Tom wasn't exactly an unknown, unproven prospect as some narratives suggest, at the time Serra was a struggling football program playing in one of the toughest leagues in the state. Legendary *San Francisco Examiner* prep sportswriter Merv Harris, who lived in San Mateo at the time, saw Brady play at Serra many times and thought he was a top-flight quarterback.

In his two years starting at Serra, Brady passed for 3,514 yards and 33 touchdowns. He had 2,121 yards and 20 touchdowns as a senior. Serra didn't get into the CIF Central Coast Section play-offs in either season (going 6–4 and 4–6), so the tough competition of the West Catholic Athletic League limited Brady's number of games played and his totals in those games he did play. Harris, who died in 2005, still honored Brady as one of the top quarterbacks in the San Francisco Bay Area. It was too hard, though, to get Brady on the all-state team with so many other quarterbacks who passed for 1,000 yards or more and who were on teams that won championships.

At Serra, Brady continued to play on the baseball team. He was a catcher and not a pitcher as many would assume. Pro scouts made stops at Serra and at other schools in the WCAL and loved to watch Brady make throws to second base. He also displayed some power, with eight home runs in his two varsity seasons to go with a .311 batting average.

By the time of his high school graduation, Brady and his parents, Tom Sr. and Gaylinn, were happy he had received football scholarship offers and had signed with the University of Michigan. Still, the Montreal Expos thought they might be able to work something out and picked Brady in the 18th round of the 1995 MLB Draft.

As Brady himself tweeted 21 years later: "I was fortunate enough to be selected by the Expos in the 1995 MLB Draft. But . . . I am so happy I stuck with football! What do you guys think?"

While it wasn't easy at Michigan (especially when the Wolverines brought in Michigan high school legend Drew Henson to ostensibly be the top quarterback when Brady was still there) and he had to overcome being a sixth-round draft choice by the Patriots in 2000, Brady has since established himself as one of the greatest players in American team sports history.

"I could talk all day about him, but if I had to give the *Reader's Digest* version it's his relentless preparation," responded Dilfer when asked about Brady. "At every level, whether it's with his body, his mind, or his spirit, Tom's desire to be great is unmatched.

He's tremendously focused and he can process what's happening in front of him better and faster than anybody else."

Brady himself often jokes about his lack of athleticism compared to other quarterbacks, but that quick mind and mental preparation has been such a staple of his career that it begs a question: Is that preciseness something he was born with?

"It's all trainable," Dilfer said. "He's honed that craft and he has such a command of that craft. It's a command of the team, the game, the other team, and everything going on out there. That's what makes him great."

More on Aaron Rodgers

All the myriad quarterback combines and events, such as the Elite 11, were just getting started when Aaron Rodgers was playing at Pleasant Valley High in Chico during the 2000 and 2001 seasons. The Internet itself, with all of the recruiting sites, also was in its infancy.

Would Rodgers have been "discovered" if he had been coming up a few years later and went to a major combine? On one hand, those events make it much easier for a quarterback from a region of the state that is often overlooked by Division I college programs. And once the kids start zipping the ball around the field at those events, the ones with major college arm strength stand out like a sore thumb. But Rodgers wasn't exactly 6-foot-2 and 225 pounds as a high schooler, either. Numerous writeups have said he was 5-foot-3 as a freshman and was still well short of being 6-foot-tall as a senior.

Despite his size and the fact that he was from the CIF Northern Section, Rodgers was a State Stat Star of the Week regular and many from that part of the state recall him as one of the best players they've ever seen. Whatever the reason, colleges didn't offer. After deciding not to walk on at Illinois, Rodgers instead went to Butte College in Oroville (near Chico).

One year later and possibly two inches of growth later, Rodgers was noticed by University of California head coach Jeff Tedford. A coach who earlier in his career developed Trent Dilfer and David Carr at Fresno State into first-round picks, Tedford made a scholarship offer to Rodgers as quickly as possible. Aaron committed, he had the academics to leave Butte College after one season, and by his sophomore year he was starting in the Pac-10 Conference. By the end of that sophomore season he had 394 yards passing in a bowl game that the Bears won.

By Rodgers's junior season, he was arguably the best college quarterback in the nation and Cal had its best teams since Joe Kapp led the Golden Bears to the Rose Bowl in 1959. Ultimately, Cal didn't get to the Rose Bowl, but was 10–2. Rodgers passed for nearly 2,600 yards and 24 touchdowns and had established himself as one of the top NFL draft prospects.

At the 2005 NFL Draft, Rodgers and another California quarterback—Alex Smith from Helix of La Mesa, who had starred at the University of Utah—were both frequently mentioned as the possible No. 1 pick by the San Francisco 49ers, who had it for that year. The 49ers went for Smith, while Rodgers slipped all the way down to 24th, where he was selected by the Green Bay Packers.

Going to the Packers where he could be a backup for Hall of Famer Brett Favre and where he had plenty of time to learn the system of new head coach Mike McCarthy (hired after Rodgers's 2005 season) ended up being a great benefit for Rodgers. After Favre retired in 2008, the starting job became available and Rodgers has blossomed into arguably one of the top quarterbacks ever.

"He plays the game and makes plays in a way that makes the other all-time greats drop their jaws," Dilfer said of Rodgers, who won a Super Bowl in 2011 and despite an injury-plagued 2017 season still moved up within the all-time lists for yardage (38,000) and touchdowns (313).

More on John Elway

While Aaron Rodgers was pretty much an unknown player in high school other than in his hometown, it was exactly the opposite for John Elway. He was a Southern California wonderboy and was widely acclaimed as the top quarterback prospect in the nation.

At the time, Elway's father, Jack, was the head football coach at Cal State Northridge, a college that no longer has a program. John and his family came to Southern California after spending his freshman year in Pullman, Washington, where his dad had been an assistant coach at Washington State. Jack liked Granada Hills as somewhere Elway could succeed on the football field, because at the time the Highlanders were running an early version of the spread, passing-oriented offense under head coach Jack Neumeier.

Elway started playing varsity minutes at Granada Hills as a sophomore and by his junior season in 1977 was showing off that cannon arm of his, displaying talents that energized college coaches everywhere. As a junior, Elway passed for 3,040 yards and 25 touchdowns.

Toward the end of that season, according to the *Los Angeles Times*, Elway passed for 454 yards and four touchdowns in a zany 40–35 victory over a San Fernando High squad that was setting records of its own running the wishbone offense. He threw what was thought to be a game-winning touchdown pass with 13 seconds left, only to have that score nullified by a penalty.

Undaunted, Elway repeated the act of throwing a game-winning touchdown pass with nine seconds remaining.

Those were the years when Banning of Wilmington and its huge South Bay rivals from Carson High were very hard to beat in the CIF LA City Section. In fact, those two schools were two of the best in the state and nation. Elway had a monster outing with 479 yards passing in a 40–28 loss to Carson during his junior year and his season ended with a loss to Banning in the LA City Section semifinals. Banning went on to win the title and was the No. 1 team in the final state rankings.

By the time of Elway's senior season in 1978, he was generally viewed as the top high school college prospect in the nation and the No. 1 quarterback. There weren't recruiting networks like today, but preseason magazines, including the Street and Smith's preseason All-America teams that were done for many years by National High School Sports Hall of Fame sportswriter Doug Huff of Wheeling, West Virginia.

All of the preseason attention wasn't just because of what Elway had done as a junior on the football field. He was racking up elite totals as both a pitcher and a hitter on the baseball diamond as well.

Elway started out the 1978 season as if he was eager to prove a point. He was averaging 306 yards passing in his first five games, but then in a game against San Fernando he hobbled off the field after getting tackled. The verdict: torn cartilage in his knee. Today, those injuries get scoped and a player might only be out for two to three weeks. In that time, however, Elway had to get surgery and was lost for the season.

Despite the injury, Elway still played enough games so that he is listed as the 1978 Mr. Football State Player of the Year. The winner of that honor the previous season in 1977 was a quarterback with running back skills from San Diego named Marcus Allen. The Lincoln High grad and NFL Hall of Famer impacted Elway in a life-changing moment many years later by introducing him to his second wife, Paige Green, at a golf tournament.

One of the stranger recruiting dramas then unfolded for Elway and his family. Shortly after the season, San Jose State hired Jack to be its new head coach. San Jose State at the time was a big step up from Cal State Northridge, but it's not part of the Pac-10. Jack later proved to be a great hire for the Spartans, but there were whispers on campus that an attempt to land the son was part of why the father got the job.

Jack once joked to a reporter: "I told him if he went to San Jose State, I'd sleep with his mother."

If John had gone to San Jose State, he'd have been the greatest recruit that school has ever had. He whittled it down to Stanford and San Jose State, but Stanford got the signature. Elway would later graduate with a degree in economics.

The San Jose State-Stanford games that Elway quarterbacked in and in which his father's team was trying to beat him usually showed Janet Elway, Jack's wife and John's mom, sitting in the stands wearing a hat with one-half in Spartan colors and the other in Cardinal red-and-white. Stanford won those games in 1979 and 1980, but in John's final two seasons his father's team won twice and likely cost him Heisman Trophy votes (he finished second). Those are still two of the biggest wins in San Jose State history, but as the Spartans were hopping up and down and screaming with joy in the locker room afterward their coach could barely be heard talking to reporters. Jack said the right words, complimenting his players, but it was clear from looking in his eyes that he wasn't happy. It wasn't hard to wonder whether the father, deep down, would have rather lost to the son.

Elway wasn't done with baseball, either. In his senior year at Granada Hills, he was the most valuable player of the CIF LA City Section championships, a title that the Highlanders also won in 1978. According to the *Los Angeles Times*, Elway had nine hits in 13 at-bats during those playoffs and pitched 4⅔ innings of relief in a 10–4 victory over Crenshaw of Los Angeles in the title game at Dodger Stadium. One of the leading players at Crenshaw was No. 1 MLB Draft pick Darryl Strawberry. Elway also continued to play baseball at Stanford and was signed by the New York Yankees to play one season of minor league ball while continuing to finish up his college football career.

Elway's NFL career, as most know, was one of breathtaking success. This included three trips to the Super Bowl with the Denver Broncos as AFC champions, beginning in 1988, that were all losses. Then in 1997, Elway and his team earned its first Super Bowl crown with a win against the Green Bay Packers. In 1998, the Broncos repeated, Elway was the MVP, and his leap into the end zone on a scramble play is one of the all-time great moments of the game.

After that last Super Bowl, Elway retired from football with 300 touchdown passes and more than 51,000 yards in 16 seasons. He was able to watch his four kids with first wife Janet all grow up and play high school sports in the Denver area, but only a few years after retirement in 2001 and 2002 he suffered a pair of tragedies. In 2001, Jack was struck with a heart attack and died at age sixty-nine. Then the next year, John's twin sister, Jana, who was on the San Jose State tennis team when her brother was at Stanford, died from lung cancer at age forty-two.

In later years, Elway has become one of the top executives in the NFL. The Broncos remain his team and at the 2016 Super Bowl held not far from Stanford and San Jose State at the brand new Levi's Stadium, the Broncos beat the Carolina Panthers 24–10.

Perhaps Dilfer said it best when characterizing the play of Elway, Rodgers, and Brady.

"I really don't like to get into the all-time greatest debate, but if there was a Mt. Rushmore of the best in NFL history, I think those three would have to be on it," Dilfer declared. "Three of the truly all-time greats."

10

Getting In a Few Kicks

The best kicker in NFL history from a California high school would have to be Norm Johnson, who booted field goals, PATs, and kickoffs for 18 years for the Seattle Seahawks, Atlanta Falcons, Pittsburgh Steelers, and Philadelphia Eagles from 1982 to 1999.

Johnson, who prepped at Downey High in Southern California and then went to UCLA, ranks among the top 15 all-time scorers in the NFL with 366 field goals (out of 477 attempts) and

638 PATs (out of 644 tried). He also made a 46-yard field goal in his only Super Bowl, which came for the Steelers when they beat Dallas in 1996.

Johnson wasn't that prolific in high school, but high school kicking accomplishments can be enhanced by many factors. This includes simply being on a good team that will generate more kicking opportunities, being on a team that is so dominant that the kicker rarely gets to even try a field goal (because that team scores touchdowns all the time), and having expert kicking coaches who can help their clients become very polished at a very young age.

Still, despite all the variables, there have been a few high school kickers in the state that have made their mark in the record books. In 2012, sophomore Kevin Robledo from Westlake of Westlake Village connected for a state record 20 field goals and finished his career in 2014 with a state record 42 field goals. In 2016, Manny Berz from Citrus Hill of Perris, who ended his four-year career with 45 field goals, broke Robledo's record.

Berz came from the Kohl's Professional Kicking program and benefitted by his father, Lenny, learning all he could about the position. Perhaps the most well-known of all the kicking companies is Chris Sailer Kicking and Punting, which is based in Southern California and routinely helps place top kicking and punting prospects with college programs.

Sailer once kicked for Notre Dame of Sherman Oaks and later worked with two other Notre Dame kicking alums, Nick Folk and Kai Forbath. They began with Sailer when they were freshman in high school and both have kicked in the NFL for many years. Forbath was the kicker in the 2017 season for the Minnesota Vikings. He had a key field goal during the team's NFC playoff win over the New Orleans Saints that ended with a Hail

Mary touchdown pass that put the Vikings into the NFC title game. Forbath didn't get to kick in the Super Bowl, as Minnesota lost in its next game to eventual Super Bowl champ Philadelphia.

A kicker does not have to go through a professional kicking camp, however, in order to make their NFL dreams come true.

A great example is Aldrick Rosas, who was the kicker during the 2017 season for the New York Giants. Rosas is from the small Northern California farming community of Orland and he became the first-ever NFL player from Orland, which began playing football in 1921.

"When I first saw him kick, it was obvious he was different than anybody we're used to seeing around here," said Kevin Askeland, an Orland grad who has become a historian for the CIF Northern Section. "His leg strength was off the charts. He had something like 104 touchbacks on kickoffs and he also was playing linebacker and tight end for a very good team."

It's not like Rosas took an easy route to the NFL after that, either. After Orland, he went to Southern Oregon University, which competes in the NAIA and isn't part of the NCAA. Rosas had some opportunities there, with 25 field goals in two seasons, but after suffering a torn ACL in his knee while making a tackle in the 2014 NAIA championship game, he went back home and attended Butte College in Chico, a community college that is famous for being where Green Bay Packers quarterback Aaron Rodgers gained notice after not getting college offers as a senior in high school.

Rosas wasn't even kicking at Butte College, but his booming kickoffs for Southern Oregon were witnessed by one coach from the College of Idaho, who put Rosas on the list of possible future clients for NFL agent Derrick Fox, who has represented several other specialists over the years.

Even with no NCAA kicking experience, Rosas still shocked many former Orland teammates and others in the Chico community by declaring for the 2016 NFL Draft. Rosas and a local kicking coach he was now working out with, Abel Hernandez, made a video of him kicking and sent it to all 32 NFL teams.

It only took one bite out of the 32 for Rosas to have a chance, and it came from the Tennessee Titans. They signed him to an undrafted free agent contract and he was brought into the 2016 summer training camp. Rosas's odds of making the roster were stacked against him and he was eventually cut, but he was able to gain invaluable experience working alongside veteran Titans kicker Ryan Succup. Rosas also did just enough in those preseason games to gain the attention of other NFL teams, including the Giants.

Although Rosas wasn't signed by any team during the 2016 season, the Giants brought him in to compete for their starting

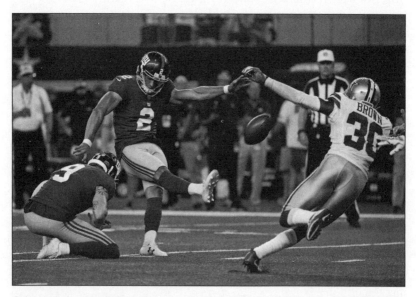

Orland High grad Aldrick Rosas won the job as the New York Giants' starting kicker in 2017. *(Associated Press)*

job for 2017. Rosas captured the job over veteran Mike Nugent after he made the game-winning 48-yard field goal in a preseason game against the New England Patriots.

"It was a dream come true," Rosas told writer Dan Duggan of New Jersey Advance Media in a 2017 article. "It was a moment of excitement. There were just a lot of feelings that I can't even explain. But I'm grateful for the opportunity."

Another recent kicker from a California high school who took a unique road to the NFL was Carmel's Andrew Franks. He went to NCAA Division III Rensselaer Polytechnic Institute in New York and kicked for that team while pursuing his undergraduate degree in Biomedical Engineering. Like Rosas, Franks did enough to gain some tryout opportunities and in 2015 and 2016 he was the regular kicker for the Miami Dolphins. In those two years, Franks made 29 of 37 field goals for the Dolphins with a longest field goal of 55 yards.

11

A Legend Among Legends

It was impossible not to listen closely at a summer football camp in the late 1990s when the two winningest coaches in California history at the time were catching up with each other. It wasn't long after Herb Meyer from El Camino High of Oceanside had surpassed Gene Vollnogle of Carson as the state record holder for most wins.

Meyer eventually retired in 2003 with 338 wins in a career that began in 1959 at Oceanside. Vollnogle, who died in 2012, retired in 1990 with 289 wins from his years both at Carson and at Banning of Wilmington. He continued to coach freshman-sophomore teams both at Carson and at Los Alamitos after he retired as a head coach.

After greeting each other and getting updated about some of the players they had coached, they began to talk about the record that Meyer held at the time and that Vollnogle had held for many years in the 1980s.

"Have you seen De La Salle play yet?" Vollnogle asked of a certain school in Northern California that had recently set a state record for longest winning streak.

"Yes, they are a machine," Meyer responded. "That coach is going to leave the rest of us in the dust."

That coach is Bob Ladouceur, who in a sense did leave all other coaches in state history in the dust during his career from 1979 to 2012. After his final game for the Concord school, which was a win over Centennial of Corona in the 2012 CIF Open Division championship game, Ladouceur's career coaching record stood at 399–24–2. He's still more than 50 wins in front of any other coach on the all-time state list and his winning percentage of 94.1 percent is by far the best among any coaches on the national all-time list who have 300 wins or more. It's also easily the best in California history for any coach with 200 wins or more.

Ladouceur, however, would be the first to react uncomfortably about any characterization of his coaching career in numbers. It was the same when his teams at De La Salle went on their legendary 151-game winning streak from 1992 to 2003 that not only broke the national record but doubled the previous record and likely is one national record that may never be broken.

"The number at 400 or 399 didn't matter one way or the other," Ladouceur said of his own retirement process. "People ask if I'm ever disappointed about not getting 400 and no, I don't ever think that."

With Ladouceur's long-time defensive coordinator and former De La Salle athletic director Terry Eidson showing no interest in being the head coach upon Ladouceur's departure, Justin Alumbaugh, a teacher at De La Salle who had been helping Ladouceur with coaching duties for more than 10 years, became Ladouceur's successor in 2013, and by 2014 and 2015 he already had his first two CIF Open Division state crowns.

"I'm just glad that [Justin] stayed for as long as he did," Ladouceur said. "He could have been a head coach somewhere else earlier. He was just brilliant even when he played for me and I remember how he never forgot a thing."

Alumbaugh was an all-state linebacker for the Spartans in 1997, which was the year that they surpassed Hudson (Michigan) to break the national win streak record. Hudson had won 72 straight games in a streak that ended in 1975 and many players from that team flew out to the Bay Area to see De La Salle win its 73rd in a row. The Spartans did, with a 56–0 triumph over College Park of Pleasant Hill and afterward Ladouceur addressed a media throng of seven TV cameras, 10 to 15 print journalists, and numerous broadcast journalists, including those from CNN, ESPN, and Associated Press.

Ladouceur had been already looking at Alumbaugh to be a future head coach—and a very good one, at that—even when Alumbaugh was in his high school and college years. In fact, as a young player, Ladouceur had benefitted from a similar experience.

After playing for San Ramon Valley of Danville and coming home after one season at the University of Utah, Ladouceur was approached by his high school coach, Fred Houston, who noticed his former player working out one day.

"This was 1972–73 and I had hair down to my shoulders," Ladouceur said. "Fred saw me and said, 'What are you doing?'"

While Ladouceur's father was trying to get a different school, San Jose State, interested in his son, Houston asked if Ladouceur might be interested in helping coach the San Ramon Valley varsity.

"I had been the team captain in my senior year and I knew the offense and defense so I thought, *Sure, why not?*" Ladouceur said. "I enjoyed it and it felt natural."

Houston remains a friend of Ladouceur's and the two eat lunch together frequently. Two of Houston's grandsons, quarterback Bart (later played at Wisconsin) and defensive tackle Sumner (later played at Oregon State), also became players for Ladouceur.

"I know Fred is very proud of me and the career I've had," Ladouceur said. "And I credit him for a lot of that success. He was a great coach."

It was still several years later after Ladouceur had graduated from San Jose State and was pursuing a career in probation when he discovered he enjoyed coaching more. He also had gone back to college at St. Mary's College in Moraga, where he was taking theology classes.

"I really wanted to get out in the field for probation, but then Prop 13 passed and I found out that wasn't going to happen for four or five more years. In the meantime, I also was coaching at Monte Vista [Danville] with a former roommate of mine, Rob Stockberger. I felt like I could do this."

After the 1978 season, an opening for varsity football coach came up at a parochial school in the area. Ladouceur saw an ad in the *Catholic Voice* newspaper, which also indicated a religion teacher was needed as well. He applied and at age twenty-four became the head football coach at De La Salle.

"Expectations were low, we didn't even have weights and all of the equipment was banged up," Ladouceur recalled. "We had to improvise, but that first year was special because we beat a couple of teams we had no business beating. We were actually an eyelash from going 8–1."

Ladouceur's first undefeated team came in 1982 at 12–0. Then in 1985, the Spartans finished 12–0 and were voted No. 1 in the state for the first time, which was for Class AAA. They had a 44-game win streak from 1984 to 1987 and were threatening the state record (47, at that time) until a 14–13 loss to Monte Vista of Danville in the 1987 CIF North Coast Section Class 4A final.

It was during this time frame when some of the most dominating players began coming to De La Salle and merged with the coaching of Ladouceur and his staff. That's why the program saw no difficulties in moving up from the Class 3A level to Class 4A. Some of those players in those years included future NFL players Aaron Taylor (offensive tackle) and Amani Toomer (wide receiver).

The national record winning streak began after a 35–27 loss to Pittsburg in the 1991 NCS championship at the Oakland Coliseum. The Spartans were 13–0 in 1992, 13–0 in 1993, 13–0 in 1994, 13–0 in 1995, and 12–0 in 1996, followed by the 1997 season in which the national record fell.

Earning consensus national No. 1 rankings and even being considered the No. 1 team in California, however, was not as easy to achieve. In those years, there were no CIF state bowl games, but beginning in 1998 the Spartans played some of the best teams in Southern California and beyond.

"People would say we were really good but didn't play anybody," Ladouceur said. "We had never ventured down south before and it was a turning point in 1998. But we also were ready for it."

That was evident in a 1998 game at Anaheim Stadium against a Mater Dei of Santa Ana team that had been voted No. 1 in the nation twice earlier in the decade by *USA Today*. The Spartans got out to a 21–7 halftime lead and held on for a 28–21 win. Mater Dei didn't lose for the rest of the season and after the Monarchs topped Long Beach Poly for the CIF Southern Section top division title there was no doubt about De La Salle's place in California.

At halftime of that Mater Dei game, NBA player Brent Barry, an alumnus of De La Salle and who went on to play for the Los Angeles Clippers, was seen cheering on the team as it exited the field. "We belong, we belong," Barry yelled. The Spartans have belonged on the state and national scene ever since.

The streak continued in 1999 when future NFL linebacker D. J. Williams was leading the team on both sides of the ball. It went on in 2001 when the Spartans beat Long Beach Poly 28–19 in the first ever No. 1 vs. No. 2 national rankings matchup and debuted a junior running back, Maurice Drew, who later led the NFL in rushing twice as Maurice Jones-Drew of the Jacksonville Jaguars. It also kept going in 2003 when ESPN featured the Spartans in the first nationally televised high school football game (they played Evangel Christian of Shreveport, Louisiana) and one of the team's top players was linebacker-tight end-running back Terrence Kelly.

Shortly before the 2004 season began, however, Kelly was murdered after a pickup basketball game in nearby Richmond just days before he was leaving to start his collegiate career at Oregon. Ladouceur wasn't sure about his own health, either, after suffering a mild heart attack earlier that spring. The team's first game was against Bellevue, Washington, in a showcase event that was played at Qwest Field in Seattle.

"We were a really young team and they were much better in person than they were on film from the year before," Ladouceur said. "After the first few times they had the ball, I thought that is a different team. I knew we were in trouble. They also bolstered their roster a little bit with a few guys they didn't have before, but that's the way it goes."

De La Salle proceeded to lose that game 38–20 and the streak was over. The Spartans then lost their next game at home to Clovis West of Fresno and after their seventh game they were only 2–3–2. One of those losses was by a close 19–17, to a Mission Viejo team that went on to finish No. 1 in the state.

In the eighth game of that season, something clicked. The Spartans played unbeaten Pittsburg and won and then in the NCS playoffs they went up against a 12–0 team from Amador Valley (Pleasanton) and pulled off an upset to keep their streak of section titles still going.

"Our first time on a bus with that [2004] team was going to a funeral," Ladouceur remembered. "Then when we were losing it was like a pall around here. They really needed to work hard but dug themselves out of it. What a triumph it was at the end. And yes, that was one of my favorite seasons because of how the kids came back."

Later in 2014, many elements of that 2004 season were included in a movie about the Spartans based on the book *When the Game Stands Tall*, written by Neil Hayes. Ladouceur was portrayed by Jim Caviezel (who earlier played Jesus Christ in a Martin Scorcese movie) while Eidson was portrayed by Michael Chiklis (who also once played the Incredible Hulk). That movie also included the famed Long Beach Poly game from 2001 and scenes that Hayes wrote about from the 2002 season.

Bob Ladouceur is shown in January of 2013 after he officially announced his retirement as head football coach at De La Salle. *(Harold Abend)*

Caviezel was on the sidelines watching the Spartans defeat Centennial in 2012 in what turned out to be Ladouceur's final game. The team didn't completely bounce back from the dip it suffered in 2004 until 2007 when the Spartans ended an unbeaten season with a 35–31 victory against Centennial the first time they played that school. The Huskies got revenge in 2008 by topping De La Salle, but then in 2009 the Spartans started a run of four straight CIF Open Division state title victories. During those four years of playing the best team from Southern California, the Spartans had a hard-to-believe 132–8 scoring margin during one span of 17 quarters. This was from the second half of the 2009 game through the first half of 2012.

Later in the 2010s, other California schools have emerged and arguably have surpassed De La Salle on the national spotlight in terms of rankings. But what Ladouceur, Eidson, and other longtime assistants such as Joe Aliotti and Mark Panella have accomplished doesn't just rank as the most impressive in state history but nationally.

"It's a culture that you have to cultivate," replied Ladouceur the coach when asked how the team stays so focused from one game to one season at a time. "You have to have talented coaches who recognize the fundamentals. We've never had anything to hide. You have to beat them with fundamentals—one step, one block at a time.

"We all knew [at the beginning] it was going to be a process. It was all going to start up front with average guys you take to the next level. And we always knew it was going to take from January to December."

12

From Sanger to the Super Bowl

As a senior in high school in the middle of the 1950s, Tom Flores can remember when a new high school football stadium was being built in his hometown of Sanger, an agricultural community with deep roots in the railroad industry that is located 13 miles southeast of Fresno in California's San Joaquin Valley.

"The farmers would come in with these backhoes and they'd start chewing up the dirt," the 80-year-old Flores said during a phone interview in the summer of 2017. "People from all over the area would show up to help."

Today, that stadium is still used by Sanger High football teams and the name on the front of it is still proudly shining under the Friday night lights: Tom Flores Stadium.

And why wouldn't Sanger have named its stadium for Flores? He wasn't just a head coach of an NFL team that won a pair of Super Bowls. Flores also will forever be known as the first Latino starting quarterback in professional football and the first minority head coach to win a Super Bowl. He's also one of just two people—the other is former Chicago Bears' head coach Mike Ditka—to win a Super Bowl as a player, as an assistant coach, and as a head coach.

Those are all amazing accomplishments, but it's how Flores came up from that upbringing in Sanger to overcome obstacles all along the way that should be inspiring for young athletes not just in his hometown but from throughout California.

"When I was growing up there, I always loved sports, but actually my favorite sport was basketball, baseball was second, and football was third," he said. "I just went out for football to be with my friends and volunteered to play quarterback in my sophomore year."

Flores's brother, Bob, was older and also was a quarterback, so the younger brother wasn't eager to compete for the same position.

"The coaches kept asking and realized that's where I belonged. I always knew I could throw the ball and in class I'd be sitting there drawing up plays."

One of the luckiest breaks that Flores did have in his high school career was being at Sanger within the same window as head coach Clare Slaughter. He was only there for five years from

1950 to 1955 before he went on to become a head coach at Fresno City College where he won four state championships during a legendary 20-year career.

At Sanger, Slaughter was innovative at the time in the passing game and Flores wasn't the only top quarterback at the school. The Apaches also had Nick Papac, who was a year older and who later played at Cal and at Fresno State.

"When I was a junior, he was a senior and I was his backup," Flores said. "The amazing thing is that years later in 1961 Nick became my backup with the [Oakland] Raiders."

Flores didn't have many four-year college opportunities, so he went to Fresno City College to gain experience and develop his skills. There were few options after he played for the Rams as well, but Slaughter had success at University of the Pacific in Stockton, so Flores decided to go there on an academic scholarship.

"I liked the way it worked out because at Pacific we had good teachers and that's what good coaches are—they teach," Flores said. "I liked the smallness of the campus and the intimacy, but we played big schools. That breeds better discipline."

Flores continued to play football for the Tigers and became a standout for head coach Jack "Moose" Myers. In the 1958 and 1959 seasons, they went 11–6–3 with Flores as the starting quarterback. He passed for 2,099 yards and 19 touchdowns.

Just as after high school and JC ball, however, Flores had a difficult time breaking into professional football. He didn't make the roster in attempts with the Calgary Stampeders of the Canadian Football League and with the Washington Redskins of the NFL. He was actually working as an assistant coach at UOP when he got a call from the Raiders. At the time, they were playing in the American Football League and Flores signed to play for them three years before future owner Al Davis had even become head coach.

"Al was incredible," said Flores of his former boss, who died at age 82 in 2011. "He could look into the future and see what was coming. And the AFL changed the way the game is played. We were doing wide open, crazy stuff all the time."

Flores played seven seasons for the Raiders before he was traded to the Buffalo Bills. He played there for three years and then became the backup to starting quarterback Lenny Dawson of the Kansas City Chiefs in 1969. That year, the Chiefs went to the fourth Super Bowl ever played and defeated the favored Minnesota Vikings 23–7.

As a player, Flores wound up with 11,969 yards and 93 touchdowns in 10 AFL seasons. He had one year with the Bills when he threw for 2,638 yards and 24 TDs. Still, it was a playing career that wouldn't come close to what he'd do later as a coach.

The Raiders weren't the organization that Flores began coaching with—that was Buffalo—but only a few years after retiring as a player he was a top assistant in Oakland under then head coach John Madden.

In 1977, Madden and the Raiders finally got over the hump in reaching and then winning in the Super Bowl. They defeated the Vikings 32–14 in a game played at the Rose Bowl in Pasadena.

After Madden retired in 1979 and soon began his legendary broadcasting career, Flores was handed the reins as the new head coach. Although several top players had retired from the team that won the Super Bowl after the 1976 season, including Hall of Fame quarterback Kenny Stabler, Flores combined with quarterback Jim Plunkett (a graduate of James Lick High in San Jose) to take the Raiders back to the Super Bowl after the 1980 season. They played the Philadelphia Eagles in New Orleans and won for the second time in five years, this time by 27–10.

Flores then had to coach amid the uncertainty about where

Oakland Raiders head coach Tom Flores and quarterback Jim Plunkett worked together to lead their team to a win in the Super Bowl in 1981 over the Philadelphia Eagles. Flores is from Sanger. Plunkett is from James Lick High (San Jose). *(Associated Press)*

the Raiders were going to play. Davis wanted to move the team from Oakland to Los Angeles after the 1980 season, but had to battle forces in the league office. Eventually, Davis moved the Raiders to LA after the 1982 season.

All of the Super Bowls that Flores was involved in were different in many ways, but one constant is that they were all wins and none of the games were close. That was true as well for the 1984 Super Bowl in Tampa. With MVP Marcus Allen (a Lincoln High of San Diego grad) leading the way with a virtuoso performance at running back, Flores and the Raiders blew out the Washington Redskins 38–9.

"When you've been in the Super Bowl before as a player you obviously know what to expect," Flores said. "Lenny Dawson was the starter and MVP when I played, but I knew what we were supposed to do. Then as an assistant coach, I saw all that had to be done.

"My first one as a head coach was a lot of the same from a few years earlier, but now you're the guy involved in everything. The games just kept getting bigger and bigger. When you're in it, there's not much of a chance to enjoy it. Some of those years (other than practice) I never left the hotel."

Flores stopped coaching the Raiders after the 1987 season. He later spent three years as head coach of the Seattle Seahawks from 1992 to 1994 and retired from coaching with a 97–87 record and an 8–3 record in the postseason.

"What I did in coaching was I took what I thought was the best parts and worst parts of all my experiences and then tried to develop the best parts and avoid the worst," Flores said. "Football is an incredible team game in which you all have to depend on so many others."

After his coaching career, Flores has spent most of his time in the Palm Springs area with his wife Barbara, who he met when the two were at UOP. They have two twin sons, a daughter, and grandchildren. He's also stayed firmly connected to the Raiders fan base by doing radio commentary at games for many years.

It was while getting ready for a Sunday NFL game during the 2016 season in the Raiders' locker room on a Saturday when Flores was approached by starting quarterback Derek Carr.

"Someone came up from behind me and said, 'Hey, Sanger is undefeated, Sanger is undefeated,'" Flores recalled. "It was Derek. He wanted to make sure I knew. In the midst of a playoff run we were in and here he is talking about high school football. But that is the kind of kid that he is. It's never about himself."

Carr has a connection to the San Joaquin Valley as well. He graduated from Bakersfield Christian in 2008 and during that 2016 season the team that his brother, Darren, coaches also was undefeated heading into the CIF state bowl games. Neither Sanger or Bakersfield Christian would win state titles, but the connection between the old head coach and the up-and-coming star quarterback was easy to see.

"I was at a game in Sanger that season and I've followed them a lot over the years," Flores said. "Chuck Shidan [who retired after 2016 with more than 200 career wins] did a fabulous job coaching them."

Flores has maintained a gritty, get-it-done attitude even in his broadcasting career. After attending an event at AT&T Stadium in Dallas in conjunction with a trip by the Raiders to play the Cowboys in a preseason game, Flores took a spill in a hallway and suffered a sprained neck, had to get 13 stitches from a cut on his face, and missed two games. He returned to the booth wearing a neck brace and finished the 2017 season.

"All of that which I achieved in football came from a certain toughness," he said. "My dad showed me that. He didn't know what a football was [coming to California from Mexico at age 12]. But he just rolled up his sleeves and went to work."

More Super Bowl-Winning Head Coaches from the Golden State

Tom Flores said he never thought about the numerous other head coaches in the NFL who won Super Bowls and like him were from California high schools. He did have an answer, however, as to why he thought there were so many.

"I played quarterback and quarterbacks like to be innovative," he said. "People from California also are innovative."

The head coach of the Raiders who won the team's first Super Bowl in 1977, John Madden, is one of those coaches. He is from Jefferson High in Daly City.

And speaking of innovative, perhaps the most innovative of all NFL head coaches who've ever donned a head set, Bill Walsh, is also from California. Walsh went to Washington High in Los Angeles, but graduated from Hayward High in the Bay Area. He won Super Bowls while head coach of the San Francisco 49ers in 1982, 1985, and 1989.

Walsh's successor, George Seifert, kept the streak going as head coach of the 49ers when they won Super Bowls in 1990 and 1995. Seifert is from the now closed Poly High of San Francisco.

The only other California high school grad to win multiple Super Bowls as an NFL head coach is Joe Gibbs. He is from Santa Fe High of Santa Fe Springs and guided the Washington Redskins to world championships in 1983, 1988, and 1992. Gibbs has gone on to build one of the most successful NASCAR racing teams in that sport's history.

Others on the list in addition to Flores, Madden, Walsh, Siefert, and Gibbs would be Mike Holmgren from Lincoln of San Francisco (1997 Green Bay Packers), Dick Vermeil of Calistoga (2000 St. Louis Rams), Brian Billick of Redlands (2001 Baltimore Ravens), and Pete Carroll from Redwood of Larkspur (2014 Seattle Seahawks).

The last head coach from California to reach the Super Bowl was Ron Rivera of the Carolina Panthers, who is from Seaside (Monterey County). Rivera's team lost in the 2015 game to the Denver Broncos, but during a press conference before the game he was asked about being just the second Latino head coach to lead a team to the biggest stage in American sports.

"Don't forget about Tom Flores," Rivera told reporters. "He's a pioneer.

"If you coach this game and have the level of success he had, you should have the opportunity (to be in the Hall of Fame). He really should."

13

Deaths, Head Injuries, and Concussions

According to a report from the Centers for Disease Control and Prevention issued in January of 2017, there were 28 deaths from traumatic brain and spinal cord injuries reported between 2005 and 2014 in the United States among the more than one million participants in football at the college and high school levels. That's an average of 2.8 deaths per year. Four of those cases were from college, 20 from high school, and the rest at other levels of the game (including junior college).

Of course, all those statistics fail to tell the stories of the young men involved. Years later, the school communities in which these deaths from head injuries have taken place still feel the impact. The coaches, players, and families will never forget.

None of these reports, either from the CDC or those from the National Center for Catastrophic Sport Injury Research, break down which states may have the highest number of incidents. In California, based on media reports over the last 22 years, there have been two in 1996, one in 1998, one in 2001, one in 2004, one in 2005, and one in 2013. There were none in 2014, 2015, 2016, and 2017.

The reports reference those cases in which a player died after incurring a head injury in a game or practice. They don't include any situations in which a player had suffered a heart attack or suffered from heat exhaustion, and they don't include any cases that may occur during the 2018 season or beyond.

With just one reported death from a head injury in the last 12 years, does that mean that in California all of the attention paid on tackling with the head up and on other concussion protocols is making a huge difference? It's too early to tell, and everyone involved—from coaches to administrators to CIF officials—will say that the concussion issue in football should not only continue to be a priority but become even more of one in the future.

That last reported death in California took place in August of 2013 in Riverside. Tyler Lewellen was a popular sixteen-year-old junior playing free safety in a three-way scrimmage on August 23 against Fontana and Rubidoux of Riverside. There was a play in which Tyler made a long run from his position and was involved in the tackle, receiving "a glancing blow" from a shoulder pad.

He briefly talked to a coach and walked to Arlington's team area, before he collapsed and went into convulsions. He was taken to a local hospital where he underwent brain surgery, but five days later he died.

Doctors later told Tyler's family that he succumbed to "severe head trauma." Two years later, his mother, Tina York, was reported to have sued the helmet maker and helmet reconditioning company for what the *Press-Enterprise* (Riverside) reported was "reason to know that the helmet was defective but failed to warn anybody." It's not known what happened after that lawsuit was filed.

In almost all cases in which such a trauma occurs on a field or court, the teams and schools involved vote to continue their seasons. And almost all of them do that for what is usually the same reported reason—that the player would have wanted them to keep playing, not missing one week of being on the field together.

When Arlington played its first official game of that 2013 season, all the media that were there noticed the same weather occurrence in the sky above the home bleachers—a rainbow had developed. The game against Chino Hills began, but from the cheerleaders to the band and for both teams it was hard to think about anything else but Lewellen.

Players wearing decal stickers with the number of a fallen teammate from a head injury hadn't happened in California since September of 2005. People at East Union High in Manteca, however, will always remember Matthew Zaragoza Van Gelderen.

Matthew was a junior defensive back and his twin sister, Katrina, was in uniform as well as a cheerleader. On a second quarter kickoff return during East Union's game at Bear Creek High in Stockton, Van Gelderen ran into a Bear Creek player. According to newspaper reports, Matthew's head collided with the other player's chest, but his mother, Zona, later told the *Record* (Stockton) that "the hit was anything out of the ordinary." Matthew raised his arms, fell back onto the field, and essentially never moved again. He died one week later at a local hospital.

Another common thread among these head injury-related deaths is the choice by families to donate the organs of their loved ones to others in need. Matthew's heart, lungs, liver, and kidney were all used in four separate transplants. His parents still speak to local high schools about the importance of having donation wishes stamped on drivers' licenses.

Only one year before Van Gelderen's death, the community of Vallejo near the Bay Area experienced a similar loss. Michael Pennerman, a junior at Bethel High, was playing in a football game at venerable Corbus Field against Rodriguez of Fairfield. There was a botched snap on one play in which Michael picked up the ball and was tackled. Unlike Van Gelderen's case, he did get up and walked to the sideline, where he began to have breathing issues and collapsed. Twelve hours later at John Muir Hospital in Walnut Creek, Pennerman died. Media reports were all consistent in writing that "traumatic brain injury" was the cause of death.

All these cases are unfathomable to any parent, but what happened to Eric Hoggatt, a senior running back at Reseda High in the CIF LA City Section, who died in 1996, seems most uncommon. Hoggatt played for the Regents during a game against Chatsworth on September 12, during which he suffered a brain injury. But unlike in the other cases, Hoggatt was allowed to go home, where he went to bed that night. When Eric's mother went to wake him up for school the next morning, he was gone.

Hoggatt's case might have ended differently given the increased knowledge these days about concussions and brain injury. According to media reports, he was allowed to go home on the team bus despite telling a volunteer doctor he had some dizziness and numbness in the fingers and legs.

Just nine days after Hoggatt's death, the Southern California prep football community was saddened by a similar incident in Orange County. This time it was a non-league football game at Newport Harbor High in Newport Beach between visiting Coronado and Costa Mesa. According to media reports at the time, Coronado was trailing 36–3 in the fourth quarter when senior quarterback Adrian Taufaasau was tackled by three or four players during a running play. He was knocked unconscious and didn't wake up again. Two days later, on a Sunday, Adrian died at Western Medical Center in Santa Ana.

A memorial to honor Taufaasau was erected near the scoreboard at Coronado, and in 2016 that memorial was refurbished by a local Eagle Scout.

Following the two deaths in 1996 and the aforementioned from 2013, 2004, and 2005, the other two brain injury-related high school football deaths in the state between 1996 and 2017 came in 1998 and 2001.

Junior linebacker Scott Maughan of Chino High was the victim in 1998. In his case, the injury didn't occur during a scrimmage or an actual game. He suffered a helmet-to-helmet hit during a tackling drill as the Cowboys were preparing to start the season in early September. Scott reportedly walked past his coaches after getting hit before showing wobbly signs and collapsed. He died at a local hospital the next day. Maughan had been a promising player and one of just two sophomores who played on Chino's 1997 CIF Southern Section Division IV championship team.

Three years later, in 2001, Costa Mesa High, which had experienced Taufaasau's death as the host school just five years earlier, unfortunately experienced tragedy from the other perspective. The Mustangs were playing Ocean View of Huntington Beach in a late September contest at Westminster High. Senior defensive end Matt Colby barreled into other players from Westminster as that team was returning the opening kickoff. He stayed in the game for two defensive plays, but then came to the sidelines and said he "wasn't feeling right," as head coach Dave Perkins told the *Los Angeles Times*. The Colby family said in subsequent statements that they knew Matt wasn't coming back just a few hours after he fell unconscious. He was kept alive by respirators so his organs could be donated.

RIP Junior Seau

It seems so routine these days to see players of Polynesian and Samoan descent playing multiple positions on top teams in the NFL, in college, and at leading California high schools. If there's been one player to lead the way, it's been California's Junior Seau, the first player of Polynesian and Samoan descent to be inducted into the Pro Football Hall of Fame.

The tragedy with Seau, of course, is that his Hall of Fame induction in 2015 was done posthumously. He had died in 2012 at his condo just off the beach in Oceanside, the community where he grew up. His girlfriend found him with what appeared to be a self-inflicted gunshot wound to the chest. He was just forty-three years old.

Seau had suspected that his depressions and outbursts of anger—there was a domestic violence arrest in 2010—were the result of him having Chronic Traumatic Encephalopathy (CTE). Because he shot himself in the chest, his brain could be studied later. Doctors from organizations looking into CTE wouldn't release any results, but the Seau family did in 2013 and confirmed that his brain showed definite signs of CTE.

For those who may not be that familiar with CTE or who didn't watch the movie starring Will Smith (whose son played football at Oaks Christian of Westlake Village), it is a disorder that develops in the brain due to the repetitive hits the brain can suffer while someone is playing football, getting hit as a boxer, or going for headers in soccer, among other such activities.

For 19 years, Seau played football in the NFL as one of the best linebackers ever and probably the best linebacker to ever come from a California high school.

Just days before the 1990 NFL Draft, Seau was at a photo shoot in the sand at Laguna Beach. It was for the first-ever *Cal-Hi Sports Magazine* (later changed to *Student Sports Magazine*). He was coming off an All-American season at USC and knew there was a chance that his hometown San Diego Chargers might pick him. They went fifth that year in the first round and probably rejoiced in the draft room when Junior was still on the board and it was their turn to pick.

Seau played 13 seasons for the Chargers and became iconic for the football team in much the same way that Tony Gwynn (Long Beach Poly grad) had done so for the Padres in baseball. In the 1994 AFC title game at Pittsburgh, Seau had a game for the ages, registering 16 tackles despite playing with a pinched nerve in his neck. The Chargers won and although they lost in the Super Bowl two weeks later to the San Francisco 49ers, the legacy of Seau as one of the toughest players in football had been firmly established.

Seau played three subsequent seasons with the Miami Dolphins and four more with the New England Patriots, including 2009, when they were undefeated all the way through to the Super Bowl before they were stunned by the New York Giants. He'll be forever known as a Charger, however, and his death in 2012 was heart-breaking to many in the San Diego community.

With his career in the books, including 10 Pro Bowl selections and a selection to the NFL's All-Decade Team for the 1990s, Seau then turned his attention toward his family. He would go to his daughter's (Sydney) volleyball matches and he'd watch his sons (Jake and Hunter) play football. Sydney and those two brothers were born during the marriage of Junior to Gina DeBoer, from 1991 to 2002. Junior's oldest son, Tyler, is from a relationship prior to his marriage.

Many of Junior's nephews also are football players. In 2011, his nephew Micah was one of the top players at Bishop's of La Jolla and led the undefeated Knights to the CIF Division IV state title, where they beat Brookside Christian of Stockton 40–14. Another nephew, Ian, was a top linebacker at St. Augustine of San Diego, then went to the University of Nevada.

Junior himself didn't get the opportunity to try for CIF state titles (at least not in football), but his multi-sport career at Oceanside High is still head-turning for many longtime fans of the Pirates. In addition to racking up multiple tackles every game as a linebacker, he also played tight end on offense and led the Pirates to a 10–3 season in his senior year. That record is particularly noteworthy given that in the middle of the 1980s, football in the San Diego area was dominated by schools like El Camino of Oceanside and Vista. The Pirates were often lucky to get above .500 until Junior arrived.

At Oceanside High, Seau also played basketball and competed in track and field. He was actually one of the top hoops players in the section as a senior and was one of just five players in the entire state named to the very first Cal-Hi Sports All-State Grid-Hoop Team. In track, he claimed two straight league titles in the shot put with a personal best throw of 56 feet, 10 inches.

Since Seau's death in 2012, the Junior Seau Foundation has

become much more involved in the research toward brain injury and CTE in football players. The foundation already had been established during Junior's NFL days to support underprivileged children and still does work toward those goals in addition to the new direction. In 2017, the Junior Seau Foundation donated $250,000 to UC San Diego for brain injury research and education. For more information on the foundation still going strong in Junior's memory, call 619-264-5555 or visit @JuniorSeauFoundation on Twitter and Facebook.

RIP Kevin Copeland

All player deaths are equally awful, especially for the families and schools involved. Among those players from the state who have died in games from heart-related issues, Kevin Copeland from Dorsey of Los Angeles certainly was one of the most publicly recognizable.

Copeland just happened to be one of the top wide receiver prospects in the nation and was one of those high school athletes in interviews and interactions that displayed a genuine interest in everyone else.

Copeland, who also was expected to be one of the top hurdlers in the nation in track and field for the spring of 1990, came up at Dorsey under then head coach Paul Knox before the Dons began to send many top players to major colleges and the NFL. Copeland's father, Ron, was an NCAA champion hurdler himself at UCLA but died after suffering a heart attack at the young age of twenty-eight.

Dorsey traveled to Daniels Field in San Pedro for a game against the host Pirates on October 6, 1989. During the second quarter, Copeland was reportedly talking to one of his coaches when he simply fell over. Trainers knew it was dire rather quickly and called paramedics. Copeland was taken to San Pedro Peninsula Hospital where he was pronounced dead at 9:30 p.m. Doctors and nurses spent nearly 45 minutes trying to save him.

Even in the age before social media, news of Copeland essentially dying on the field in front of his teammates, cheerleaders, and others from the Dorsey community spread like wildfire. On the eleven p.m. news broadcasts in one of the nation's biggest media markets, Copeland's death was the lead story. That wasn't just because of the almost surreal circumstance. It was because Kevin was so promising as an individual in everything he did.

Dorsey went on to play its season with what became known as "DDP" or Dorsey Don Pride. University of Washington running back Beno Bryant, who just graduated from the school, wore the initials on his shoes during a game against USC at the LA Coliseum. Suddenly, several others were replicating Bryant's actions.

A talented sophomore two years behind Copeland at Dorsey was a wide receiver named Keyshawn Johnson. He looked up to Copeland, and after Copeland died Keyshawn doubled up his efforts to follow in Kevin's path. Several years later, Johnson was the top pick in the 1996 draft by the New York Jets.

(Author's Note: Though I wasn't able to speak to Keyshawn for this book, I met him a couple of times later on and know that Copeland was someone who inspired him).

Johnson, who later became an ESPN on-air talent for NFL pregame shows, played in the NFL for eleven seasons. He was on a Super Bowl championship team in 2003 with the Tampa Bay Buccaneers and he finished with more than 10,000 career receiving yards and 64 touchdown catches.

A mural was painted on the Dorsey campus in memory of Copeland that is still a focus for every player who's played and attended school there.

Unfortunately, other players have suffered a similar fate to that of Copeland. Most recently, Kevin Telles of Garden Grove died of a heart-related trauma in 2009. He was one of the top players for his team and will never be forgotten.

14

Referees Can Go to the Pros Too

A casual catch in the backyard, time spent working on a car
in the garage, or trips to the movies to see the latest super-
hero flick are what many deem typical father-son experiences. For
NFL referee Pete Morelli, some of his fondest memories with his
dad (also named Pete) took place while attending local high school
football games in the early 1960s.

For the Morellis, they weren't just going to games as spectators.

Pops was in a referee's uniform and the young son loved to see the impact his dad had on games by calling or not calling penalties and helping to maintain the flow of the action.

Morelli turned sixty-six during the 2017 season, and his father died at age eighty-six in 2004. But those early experiences of watching his father helped craft a long career of refereeing football games for himself, including 15 years in the NFL as of 2017.

Referees at California high school football games—like those at all levels of the game—are mostly taken for granted. But the fact of the matter is, they have to be qualified to be on the field, which is one of the reasons there's a shortage of referees that can be assigned to games.

"Yes, there's a big shortage," Morelli said in a summer of 2017 interview. "A lot of the older guys are retiring and not a lot of young men or young women are getting into it. Not all games will be able to be played on Friday nights in the future just to accommodate this lack of officials. We'll see more and more JV games having to be played the night before."

Morelli knows about high school football because for 25 years, in addition to pursuing referee assignments in college and the NFL, he was the principal and president at St. Mary's High in Stockton.

For 99 percent of the time, Morelli was able to keep those two worlds completely apart, but there was that one occasion in 2014 when he was photographed giving a hug to Tampa Bay Buccaneers running back Doug Martin before a game. Social media blew up with the image of a referee hugging a player, but it quickly died down when people learned it was an exchange between a player and his former high school principal. Martin graduated from St. Mary's in 2007 before going to Boise State and then in 2012 and 2015 he was one of the leading rushers in the NFL.

"I've had Doug for three games and he's never had a great game in any of them," Morelli recalled, with a chuckle. "Whenever there has been an opportunity to see a player from Stockton I've always gone up to them."

Morelli himself played football at St. Mary's for four years and in his senior year the program began to turn around under new coach Duane Isetti. By 1971, just after Morelli graduated, the Rams were 9–0 and ranked among the best teams in Northern California. They only lost one game in Pete's senior season.

Morelli chose to attend college at St. Mary's College in Moraga, where he continued to play sports (football, baseball) and began to think about a career as an educator.

It was while Pete was in college that his father and his uncles Joe and Tony were forming a crew to officiate local high school games.

"I saw how much respect they got and being a player myself I thought it would be fun and I decided to do it," Morelli said. "I started at the lowest level, holding the chains and doing JV games, but I was kind of quick with the rules."

Since Morelli began with his father's crew at just nineteen years old, he learned quickly. His father and uncles also encouraged him to take more responsibility and by the time he was twenty-one he was already "wearing a white hat," which means he was the head referee for a crew himself.

"I later became involved in our local association where I was president of rules and later president," he said. "And still to this day some of the most fun I've had as an official was doing those high school games. I remember all the teams at towns like Tracy. There weren't as many schools like they have now so the quality of play was really good. I always seemed to do the big games, [CIF Sac-Joaquin] section finals and Thanksgiving Day games. My final high school game was a playoff game at UC Davis."

By the middle of the 1980s, Morelli was looking for new challenges and was brought into the Big West Conference to do college games. He then joined the Western Athletic Conference and continued to get strong evaluations in all roles, including referee.

"In the WAC is where I was noticed from the NFL," he said. "They followed me around for 12 of 14 games scouting me."

But becoming an NFL referee requires more than a positive scouting evaluation. Candidates have to pass FBI background checks and undergo psychological profiles and there are physical tests too.

Morelli got his call from the league in 1997 and was a back judge/field judge for five years before being promoted to referee prior to the start of the 2003 NFL season.

In the meantime, while chasing all of these refereeing assignments, Morelli was also gaining more responsibility as an educator and helping his wife Cindy raise their sons Matt and Dan.

In all of the years that he has been an NFL referee prior to the 2017 season, Morelli vowed that he would always report to work at St. Mary's as the principal/president on Monday.

"I had the opportunity to work with a lot of good people at the school," said Morelli, who retired from his school job in June of 2017. "You also have to be extremely organized. I couldn't waste a minute of the day doing both jobs during the season."

On a typical Friday during those years, Morelli would start with regular classes, followed by football at night. He'd then have to get up early to get to the airport on Saturday morning to fly out to whichever city was hosting the Sunday NFL game he was assigned. That evening, the officiating crew typically meets to watch film and discuss assignments and a game plan. On Sunday, game times could range from one p.m. on the East Coast to one p.m. on the West Coast, with the occasional game on Sunday

Pete Morelli completed his 21st year as an NFL referee at the conclusion of the 2017 regular season. *(Associated Press)*

night. Morelli would then typically fly home immediately after the game so he would be back at St. Mary's on Monday.

Some of the most difficult times were when St. Mary's was playing a championship game on a Saturday. Morelli was able to see the game in 2004 when the Rams won their first CIF Sac-Joaquin Section title with a 50–45 win over Nevada Union of Grass Valley. He was on the road, however, in 2008 when they played in their first CIF state final, a 37–34 loss to Cathedral Catholic of San Diego.

"I didn't miss many home games in the last 30 or so years, but toward the end [of being principal] I wouldn't go on the road that much," he said. "It's helped that we have our own radio station at St. Mary's so I could listen on the computer."

There are more and more referees these days who are actually on the radio and on TV broadcasts explaining the close calls, as replay has become more and more crucial to the game. Perhaps the most successful and entertaining among all of them is Stockton native Mike Pereira of FOX Sports. He even traveled to the biggest games in 2017 with FOX's No. 1 team of Joe Buck and Troy Aikman and sat in the booth with them.

Pereira has been critical of calls that Morelli has made on the air, so it may not be obvious that the two have a family officiating history that spans the generations. Pereira went to Stagg High in Stockton (not St. Mary's), but his own father, Al Pereira, got into football officiating in the 1950s through a connection with Morelli's father.

"Al was a high school official in the area who kept pushing me and got me started in a JC conference," Morelli continued. "But way before that, my father started Al."

Mike Pereira didn't spend as many years doing high school games, and by 1982 he already was calling college games. Then by 1996, he was in the NFL. Two years later, he was promoted to NFL supervisor of officials, and in 2004 he became the league's Director of Officiating. Pereira retired from the NFL after the 2009 season and by 2012 had started a media career.

"I refereed with Mike on his crew in the WAC," Morelli said. "He was very innovative. I think he was the first official to study game film to help prepare for the offenses as officials that we'd see for both teams."

Since they knew each other for so long and Pereira had ascended to a top position in the NFL, it probably helped Morelli in joining the league and becoming a referee in 2003. Yet Morelli still had to grade out high with his own crews to call any playoff games. In 2015, Morelli also was honored by the league with its annual Art McNally Award, which is given to an NFL official "who exhibits exemplary professionalism, leadership, and commitment to sportsmanship, on and off the field."

Both Morelli and Pereira also are quite active in trying to encourage more young men and women to become officials. Since 1994, Morelli has held a weekend clinic at St. Mary's for beginning officials. In 2017, Pereira started a foundation and hosted an event in which Morelli attended to "meet and greet" the next candidates into the profession.

"This is a great opportunity that helps these schools continue to do these activities for our kids," Morelli said. "Those who go into it understand that and deserve the respect of everyone. It's not easy and they're not making a lot of money."

15

The Voice of Pico Rivera

O n a typical Friday night in the fall in the Golden State, there might be more than 400 high school football games taking place. This doesn't count games that might be played on Thursday nights or teams with a week off.

Crowds at these games can vary greatly, from fewer than one hundred people present to more than 5,000 for the biggest rivalries. One constant in each of these games is the service provided by all of those people behind the scenes. This includes people who take your ticket; people who work in the press box such as announcers and videographers; people who work at the snack bar who are often trying to raise funds for other teams at the school; people who provide security; and people on the sidelines, such as trainers, administrators, and those who are on the chain gang.

Many of those behind the scenes share a strong connection to the school they are serving. They are often alums and some keep on going to the Friday night games long after their own son or daughter has played for the school.

El Rancho High of Pico Rivera has had one such alum who, though he didn't have children, has been the public address announcer at football games there since the 1960s. As Armando "Armie" Briones likes to tell the story, he loves it when he gets to meet the members of the marching band each year.

"I love being part of the school and plan to continue doing this as long as possible," Briones said during a phone interview in July of 2017. "The first thing I tell the band is that you don't know me, but you've heard me. I'm your halftime voice. Then the look they get on their faces is priceless. Some of these kids grew up at football games because it's still something fun to do for a family on a Friday night."

Briones grew up in the same neighborhood and attended the school they call "The Ranch" from 1963 to 1967. When he was just a freshman, almost by accident, he was given the opportunity to announce at a varsity basketball game, and it was a match made in heaven.

"I had started out that first year in audio and visual and did the setup for basketball games," Briones recalled. "The regular announcer said he had a sore throat and asked me to do it. The following Monday morning, I got a notice from the office. . .

thinking *What did I do wrong?* The principal, vice principal, and activities director were all there. They said, 'How would you like to do basketball?'"

For the rest of that 1963–64 season, Briones was the regular announcer. He sat directly behind the official scorer, but then for the 1964–65 season he became the scorer and served in both roles. He's been sitting in that chair ever since.

Announcing for the El Rancho football games was a role that Briones didn't secure until his graduation day in 1967. This was primarily because he also was in the Dons' marching band, but that changed when the principal approached him at graduation practice and asked if he wanted to announce the football games for the upcoming season. The principal said Armie could think about it but needed to know the next day at graduation.

"I handed him my name card and told [the principal] yes and then walked off the stage," Briones said.

Briones completed his 50th season announcing in 2017.

Soccer is another sport in Briones's blood as a referee and announcer. He's announced for CIF Southern Section soccer championships since 1993 and has a done a few CIF Southern California regional finals when those games were held at a neutral site.

But despite all the years of announcing at El Rancho, Briones never considered a career in broadcasting. It's always been a way to stay connected to his high school and give something back to all those generations of Pico Riverans who have followed him.

"People come up to the press box all the time who I went to school with," remarked Briones, who retired in 2007 after a 29-year career working as a pharmacy technician with Kaiser Permanente. "And now we're starting to see grandchildren of some of those people at the games."

Armie Briones and his late wife, Terry Myers Briones, were honored several years ago for their more than 50 years of work at El Rancho High football games. *(Courtesy Briones Family)*

Briones also has maintained a family atmosphere while he's announcing. His sister, Irene, has been sitting next to him for the past six years doing the team's stats while his brother, Arnold, has been at his side serving as the spotter for 35 years.

In the years since Briones began, El Rancho's football fortunes have ebbed and flowed. There have been two CIF Southern Section championship teams and one team that finished 0–10.

But the best team at El Rancho in all the years Briones has been at the school was the one in 1966—the year before he started announcing football. That one happened to feature many of his classmates who gathered in October of 2017 for a 50th reunion.

Guided by head coach Ernie Johnson, who died at age eighty-seven in 2013, El Rancho's 1966 squad never trailed for the entire season. The Dons won the CIFSS top divisional title with a 35–14 triumph against Anaheim. They were so dominant, with a 516–68 scoring advantage, that the National Sports News Service crowned them as mythical national champions.

When Briones began announcing the games in the 1967 season, El Rancho pushed its winning streak to 23 games before Anaheim got some revenge with a 28–14 playoff victory. Counting all of the Dons' results for the decade of the 1960s, they also led the state with 96 wins (97 counting a forfeit).

"What I remember most about that team is that it was very strong defensively," Briones said. "My biggest thrill was being in the band [playing the drums] and marching through the (LA) Coliseum tunnel. All the vibrations were just amazing. It was all just such great fun."

Briones maintained a friendship with Johnson for many years and spoke on the family's behalf to the media after Johnson died.

"He was outstandingly fair," Briones said. "He picked on everybody. He wanted everyone who played us to think the same thing: That you haven't been hit until you've been hit by The Ranch."

While that sounds like the comment of a true fan, Briones makes a conscious effort to be an impartial announcer for both teams at every game.

"I follow the philosophy of the late John Ramsey [longtime Los Angeles pro sports PA announcer] who said the No. 1 rule was to be accurate and to not let the go-go for El Rancho override the game. Let the game take care of itself. On every play, people want to know the ball carrier, the tackler, down, and distance. I've been where it's way less neutral and I've been to other games where you hardly hear the announcer at all."

It's good that at El Rancho they do hear the announcer, and they have been hearing him for more than 50 years.

16

Inventing the Offseason

Once a football season ends in California in December, most players and coaches enjoy the holidays, sitting in front of the tube on New Year's Day watching bowl games. Then in early January, it's back to work.

Most are not training to play games for the following season. If they're not involved in another sport such as basketball in the winter or track in the spring, many of the athletes are starting an intense training period to prepare for spring and summer off-season, football-related events.

None of these events are sanctioned by the schools, but they generate interest in the media, colleges follow them to help with recruiting, and they can improve specific skills, such as footwork for linemen, long-snapping for centers, and of course all the throwing, catching, and knocking away passes in non-contact drills and games, known as 7-on-7.

In the middle of the 1990s, there were few, if any, off-season events. Then there arose the concept of using passing games with no tackling—the 7-on-7 format—to prepare players for spring practice and the ensuing season. A testing combine for high school players similar to the tests NFL teams had been using for college players also was developed. This included a 40-yard dash, a 20-yard shuttle, the vertical leap, and a strength test.

Many of these early events in the nation were organized by *Student Sports Magazine*, which was published at the time out of an office in the lower lobby of the Anaheim Hilton & Towers. (A disclaimer: Cal-Hi Sports was part of Student Sports in those days, and the author of this book was the editor of the magazine.)

Student Sports presented passing festivals at El Camino College in Torrance for several years in the 1990s and included combine testing. The first combine ever held in Northern California was in the spring of 1993 at Napa High and is perhaps best remembered by the wet, dewy grass that needed to be mowed. The second NorCal combine at St. Mary's College in Moraga in 1994 was more successful, attracting one particularly noteworthy participant from Serra High of San Mateo named Tom Brady.

Shoe companies began to develop interest in sponsoring these events. The Student Sports football combines were first sponsored by Reebok and a national tour began. Several years later,

Nike gained sponsorship and today Student Sports is primarily an events company (purchased in June of 2017 by Blue Star Sports). The Opening, a Nike-sponsored event, held each summer in Beaverton, Oregon, and the Elite 11 Quarterback Finals have become the gold standard for these off-season gatherings. Other shoe companies now have camps and combines and there are now many off-season passing club teams that go to 7-on-7 tournaments. These teams are a collection of skill players (quarterbacks, receivers, defensive backs) who don't represent their schools. They are similar to AAU club teams in basketball.

Student Sports president Andy Bark is regarded as the pioneer for creating these off-season football events. Andy played at Palos Verdes (Palos Verdes Estates) and was good enough to gain the attention of several colleges. He decided to go to the Air Force Academy in the fall of 1979 and the coach who got him there was Bill Parcells, who later became one of the most successful coaches in NFL history.

"I got into football way back when I was a little kid and the little girl sitting in front of me in first grade was the daughter of George Allen, who at the time was the head coach of the Los Angeles Rams," recalled Bark, in May of 2017. "I didn't realize it at the time but I discovered I could slow the game down. I was playing with older kids and as a ball boy at USC and UCLA I'd get out there and run around with the college players. Coaches' kids do that too and that's why I think so many coaches' kids have success. Name them all, from Brett Favre to the Mannings. They get out there with the players and it helps their mental ability to slow the game down."

For a game at Palos Verdes that Andy remembers the most, it's hard to beat that time when the Sea Kings upset super-talented Long Beach Poly 7–6 during the 1979 season.

Andy Bark has built Student Sports into one of the most significant high school sports events companies in the nation. *(Willie Eashman)*

"We ran what some may call an antiquated offense, but our head coach was the defensive coordinator and we played lights out defense—all 11 guys," Bark said. "We didn't have anyone with a college offer and we made our PAT and they missed theirs, but it was a win. I played defensive safety and remember getting a lot of interceptions those years."

Andy eventually suffered too many concussions at Air Force, which made him ineligible to become a pilot, so he transferred to the University of California. He was on the team in 1982 that scored one of the most famous touchdowns in football history—the play with the Stanford band on the field—and a friend of his from Rolling Hills High (Palos Verdes' rival), Kevin Moen, was the one who crashed into the trombone player.

After his playing days at Cal were over, Bark made attempts to play professionally with the San Diego Chargers of the NFL and San Antonio Gunslingers of the USFL. He later worked as a broadcaster doing NFL games for an Australian TV network. His boss, Rupert Murdoch, of course, gained bigger fame and fortune. The idea to publish a magazine first came to him in college when he saw teammates devouring a Texas magazine. *California Football Magazine* was born. That eventually became a high school magazine for California (*Cal-Hi Sports*) and then a national high school magazine (*Student Sports*).

"Back in those days, there were just a select number of schools that had players get scholarships," Bark said. "This is because the NCAA had limits on coaches. There were six coaches from each college and they could go out and recruit for just 10 days. It was simple math. With that kind of time to spend, why drive 30 minutes off the freeway to Palos Verdes when you can go to Long Beach and hit Long Beach Poly, Long Beach Wilson, and

Millikan all next to each other? It was the same with Carson and Banning. There was just no time."

Not only was the lack of time an obstacle, but colleges in the 1980s and early 1990s also didn't spend the resources they do now to find out about top prospects.

"At Cal one time I was looking at a guy who I knew just flat out couldn't play at the college level," Bark said. "I asked one of the coaches how and why they recruited this player and he said they were going off a list from a newspaper."

After starting the magazine and publishing comprehensive all-state teams and statewide season reviews, Bark began to see the value of using the magazine's editorial strengths into supporting an events division.

"The idea for events to help with recruiting was that things seemed so backward and the real problem was fairness," he said. "We wanted it to be fair for the kids at schools that were not from one of the select schools to have a chance. Just have one day when it's fair for everyone. That was always the goal."

Wide receiver Joey Getherall, a 5-foot-7, 140-pound receiver from Bishop Amat (La Puente), was a favorite player of Bark's in those early years of the camps and combines. Getherall clocked a 4.38 in the 40 at one of those combines and displayed enough skills to go with that speed that he eventually signed with Notre Dame and played there, too.

"Two things have changed a lot since these events have become popular," Bark said. "First, it's quarterbacks of color. Since Elite 11, that's gone up 350 percent. There are other reasons for that, but I'd like to think we helped. Second, everyone now trains for speed. Especially for receivers. If you're tough, athletic, and can catch, we have all these offenses [like the Patriots] where smaller guys can succeed. Sure, we all want to look like Terrell [Owens] but you don't have to."

With the support of Nike's Phil Knight and Bill Keller, the Student Sports-produced football events have continued to evolve and flourish. In recent years, TV shows have even been produced about the players' experiences as they first start training for the events in their junior seasons.

With the proliferation of 7-on-7 passing festivals by other promoters around the country, however, there is a growing concern about players suffering injuries in violent collisions.

"When we started with the 7-on-7s it was after it was started in college practices," Bark said. "They were started simply to prepare teams for the fall. You had to pretend there was perfect protection on every play.

"Today, there are a lot of violent collisions in competitive 7-on-7s. It's totally different. We do them at The Opening, but we really preach it's not about winning, but about good, quick reads. If you hit, you sit. Doesn't matter if you came across the country to be there. If you hit, you sit."

It's also proven true that if you shine after traveling to one of these events, you rise.

17

Family Ties

If you had to pick one team in the history of California prep football that has had the craziest set of family ties you could imagine, then you'd probably choose Oaks Christian of Westlake Village from the 2009 season.

The Lions that season featured quarterback Nick Montana, the son of San Francisco 49ers Hall of Famer Joe Montana; backup quarterback Trevor Gretzky, the son of greatest-ever hockey legend Wayne Gretzky; and receiver Trey Smith, the son of worldwide acting icon Will Smith.

There were other outstanding players on that Oaks Christian team, including powerful running back Malcolm Jones. Thanks in part to a nationally televised win over the top-ranked team from Washington in which Trey Smith caught 10 passes with his famous dad watching from the sidelines, head coach Bill Redell's squad was in contention to be in the 2009 CIF Open Division state championship game with a 13–0 record heading into the CIF Southern Section Western Division final.

After that game in Washington, there was a crowd surrounding Montana and his family and an even larger crowd surrounding Smith and his family. Possibly because it was a football game and hockey wasn't on too many people's minds, The Great One and his wife, Janet, walked off the field and toward their car unabated. Just a few months later, he was lighting the torch at the opening ceremony of the 2010 Vancouver Winter Olympics.

Unfortunately, the Lions faced another 13–0 team in that title game, which was held at Serra of Gardena. The host Cavaliers didn't have family ties like Oaks Christian, but they had three wide receivers—senior Robert Woods, senior Paul Richardson, and junior Marqise Lee—who all eventually became starters in the NFL.

A great game was expected by many in the media and it lived up to the hype. The two teams were tied 21–21 at halftime. Oaks Christian led 35–28 entering the fourth quarter, but Serra tied it up late to force overtime at 35–35. In the extra period, both teams scored, but the Lions missed their extra point. Serra's kick went through, and the Cavaliers had won 42–41.

As the Serra players jumped around the field hugging each other immediately after the game, several Oaks Christian players began walking toward them with one of their coaches. A reporter happened to be walking in the same direction right in front of them and could overhear what that coach was saying to his players:

"Well, fellas, you know why winning feels so good? Because losing feels so bad."

That person was Oaks Christian linebackers coach Clay Matthews Jr., a former NFL player and another from that team with family ties. In fact, the Matthews family, led by Clay and his brother Bruce and his son Clay III, comprise the first family of California football.

The Matthews family could be considered a California family because most of the family members have a connection with the Golden State. The patriarch, Clay Matthews Sr., is from North Carolina, but he played in the NFL in the early 1950s with the San Francisco 49ers. Matthews Sr.'s two sons also spent some early years in California. Clay Jr. was born in California but graduated from a high school in Illinois. Bruce graduated from Arcadia High in the San Gabriel Valley.

After a stellar career at linebacker for USC, Clay Jr. played from 1978 to 1996 in the NFL, a 19-year and 278-game stretch that's probably impossible for a linebacker of today. He spent most of those years with the Cleveland Browns and had more than 1,500 career tackles, one of the highest totals in league history.

Clay Jr.'s three sons have all played football, too. Kyle Matthews was a safety at USC, Clay III also played at USC and has gone on to become a top linebacker in the NFL with the Green Bay Packers, and Casey went to Oregon and has played in the NFL with the Philadelphia Eagles and Minnesota Vikings.

Bruce Matthews played at USC as well and went on to become one of the best offensive linemen in NFL history. He spent 19 years in the league and is known for having excelled at all five offensive line positions. Matthews, who ranks No. 2 in NFL history for most consecutive starts at 292, was inducted into the Pro Football Hall of Fame in 2007.

Bruce's sons grew up and went to high school in Texas, though they too have seen immense success on the field and have emerged on lists of the top high school linemen in the nation. Jake Matthews played in the Super Bowl in 2017 for the Atlanta Falcons and is one of the top young linemen in the league. Kevin was next and has been on rosters for Tennessee and Carolina. Mike was third and also was still a developing player during the 2017 season. Luke, the youngest, was an All-American high school player in 2017 from Elkins High in Missouri City, Texas.

Father-Son State Coaches of the Year

The Bruich name is synonymous with high school football success in California's Inland Empire. After the 2014 season, both Dick Bruich and his son Kurt could see their names as State Coach of the Year.

Kurt Bruich was selected as the 2014 recipient mostly because his 15–1 team at Redlands East Valley captured the CIF Division II state title with a 34–33 win over previously unbeaten Clayton Valley of Concord.

From 1977 to 1998 at Fontana and from 2000 to 2008 at Kaiser of Fontana, Dick Bruich won 292 games with four CIF Southern Section titles and two teams (1987, 1989) that were unbeaten and selected as Cal-Hi Sports State Teams of the Year. Bruich's win total was still eighth on the all-time state list six years after he retired.

Kurt led the secondary on that 1987 Fontana team, which blanked Fountain Valley 21–0 in the CIFSS Big Five Conference final and also was ranked No. 1 in the nation according to the National Prep Poll (National Sports News Service).

Dick Bruich wasn't the State Coach of the Year for 1987, but he was the choice for 1989, which was another nationally ranked powerhouse.

Kurt went on to play at the University of Redlands and then decided to become a head football coach/educator himself.

After several seasons at Cerritos High, the younger Bruich began his own Inland Empire football journey by accepting the head job in 2002 at Redlands East Valley. In the first five years that Redlands East Valley fielded teams (the school opened in 1997), the varsity win-loss record was an abysmal 1–49.

Bruich pushed the Wildcats to their first winning season in his inaugural season. Counting the win over Clayton Valley, Bruich took a 105–33–4 record for 13 seasons into the 2015 season. His teams in 2015, 2016, and 2017 continued to have winning records at 9–3, 9–3, and 6–5. The run also includes 11 league championships and several deep playoff runs.

The 2014 team at Redlands East Valley not only had to beat a 15–0 opponent in its last game, but also had to defeat a 13–0 foe, Riverside Poly, in order to win the CIF Southern Section Inland Division title and become bowl eligible.

"I don't even try to live up to my dad's accolades," Kurt told *The Press-Enterprise* (Riverside) prior to the CIF state bowl game. "What I try to live up to, and why I wanted to get into coaching, was because I saw how many of my friends he influenced when I was in high school. Boys that didn't have everything, they always felt like they were part of our family and they went on to do bigger and better things. That was why I wanted to be just like him. It had nothing to do with championships. I wanted to do what he did with people."

Besides the FoHi Steeler Slap (in which any player who drew a flag or made a mental mistake would take off his helmet and be slapped by a designated teammate), the program was most famous for its rabid fan base and smash-mouth philosophy.

The team that Kurt played on at Fontana in 1987 coached by his father was part of a streak in which the Steelers made the CIFSS playoffs for 26 consecutive seasons between 1974 and 1999.

The 1987 team epitomized Fontana's run-first philosophy as All-State tackle Chris "Yogi" Ybarra and offensive lineman Chad Barron epitomized Fontana's run-first philosophy (3,833 yards). Running back Derrick Malone (1,908 yards, 27 TDs) did most of the damage.

At that time, the Citrus Belt League was arguably the state's toughest, and only rival Eisenhower of Rialto scored more than a touchdown on the Steelers' vaunted defense in a 26–14 loss.

In a much-hyped 12–7 playoff semifinal win over all-decade (1980s) running back Russell White and Crespi of Encino, Fontana won after trailing 7–0 entering the fourth quarter. The defense slowed White in the second half after he scored on a 41-yard run on his second carry. In the 21–0 win over Fountain Valley in the section title game, the defense gave up only six yards rushing and 96 total.

Fontana repeated its title in 1989 with another steam-rolling performance in the CIF-SS major division title game. The Steelers played San Gorgonio of San Bernardino, which was led by future NFL running back Ron Rivers, and won 35–7. Samita Vaoifi helped Bruich's team overcome an early 7–0 deficit with touchdown runs of 38 and 8 yards.

"I never even dreamed about [going 14–0]," said Vaoifi to reporters after the game. "When I heard about the team two years ago going 14–0, I told myself, 'I wish I could do that.' It still feels improbable."

Dick Bruich, a native of Nebraska, was a former defensive coordinator at St. Paul of Santa Fe Springs, where he learned all the tricks of the trade from St. Paul head coach Marijon Ancich. Bruich went to Fontana as an assistant in 1975 and became the Steelers' head coach in 1977. Ancich was known for developing a number of other head coaches in his years at St. Paul. He is the second-winningest head coach in state history.

A Family of Quarterbacks

It came full circle for the Johnsons of El Toro/Mission Viejo during the fall of 2015. It was then that Mission Viejo High was in the midst of a 16–0 season that ended with a CIF Division I-AA state championship.

Senior Brock Johnson, the grandson of head coach Bob Johnson, was leading the Diablos at quarterback. Brock's dad, Bret, was the offensive coordinator, and Brock's uncle, Rob, also was one of the coaches.

As the Johnsons gathered for a family photo after that game, it was hard not to recognize the many games and events over a 30-year span at which at least one of them had coached or played.

The Johnsons have always been a family of quarterbacks. Bob played the position himself at Redondo Union High (Redondo Beach) in the early 1960s, then later at Fresno State.

"That's the position I loved and played and was just able to continue with it," Coach Johnson said during a January 2017 interview. "I would have cared less if they [sons Bret & Rob] played another position, but they were both just happy campers about that."

Bret's team at El Toro in 1986, when he was a junior, went 14–0 and was the Cal-Hi Sports State Team of the Year. The

Chargers had few weaknesses and are considered as one of the state's most outstanding two or three teams for the decade of the 1980s. They won a showdown against another highly regarded team with a highly regarded quarterback, 17–15, over Capistrano Valley of Mission Viejo. At the time, Capistrano Valley was led by Todd Marinovich—also known as "Robo QB" by some in the media due to the training he was receiving from his father, Marv. El Toro went on after that win to defeat Santa Ana 26–10 in the CIF Southern Section Western Conference championship.

As a senior, Bret didn't lose a game, either, but the Chargers were not ranked as high. Bret finished his career with 6,653 yards passing. He was selected as the 1986 Mr. Football State Player of the Year and was one of the state's best quarterbacks for the 1980s.

As Bret was then getting into his collegiate career at UCLA, Rob was coming up two years behind him. There was a complication in his development as a quarterback, however, because El Toro had another talented quarterback, Steve Stenstrom, who was one year older.

A compromise of sorts was reached between the father, the son, and Stenstrom. Rob would play receiver for his junior season while Steve would be the starting quarterback. The plan worked, as Steve was able to earn a scholarship offer from Stanford and Rob gained insight into playing the receiver position that possibly helped him as a quarterback later on.

Nevertheless, reaching that decision still wasn't easy.

"QB-wise they're both great players and both played in the pros, but it was hard because Rob is a quarterback and he's always been a great quarterback," coach Johnson recalled. "Rob knew Steve and knew it worked out well for him. Rob wouldn't say anything that season. It was a hard decision."

That one season as a receiver didn't prevent Rob from collecting major college offers, though. That was partly due to him being one of the best basketball players in Orange County and also one of the top baseball players. Johnson wasn't the 1990 Mr. Football State Player of the Year, but he had a strong season with 2,788 yards passing and 28 touchdowns. He also was the 1990–91 State Boys Athlete of the Year. One of the others under consideration for that was golfer Tiger Woods from Western High of Anaheim.

After his tenure at USC, Rob went on to play for 10 years in the NFL. Bob Johnson stepped away from El Toro after the 1990 season and he didn't return to being a head coach until the 1999 season at Mission Viejo. In the interim, he got to see his sons compete at the collegiate level.

After Rob helped USC win the Cotton Bowl Classic in 1995, he was a fourth-round pick by the Jacksonville Jaguars. He had some breakout games as a rookie replacing the injured Mark Brunell and then the following year signed a four-year, $25 million deal to become the starter for the Buffalo Bills. Rob had an up-and-down career with the Bills, primarily because he was sacked so often. He started for them in a 2000 AFC wild-card game against the Tennessee Titans and drove them to what many thought would be a game-winning field goal with 16 seconds left. The Titans then pulled off what became known as the Music City Miracle on the ensuing kickoff return and beat the Bills 22–16.

After his time with the Bills, Rob played as a backup for two years with the Tampa Bay Buccaneers and earned a Super Bowl ring when the Bucs beat the Oakland Raiders in the 2003 Super Bowl. He later added backup stints with the Raiders and Washington Redskins. Throughout his career, Rob passed for 5,795 yards with 30 touchdowns and 23 interceptions.

Bret finished up his collegiate career at Michigan State and then later played in the Canadian Football League for the Toronto Argonauts. He also gained some experience playing in the NFL for the Atlanta Falcons.

With their father ending his coaching career after the 2017 season with 342 wins, it's evident that had it not been for the eight seasons that Bob Johnson was inactive from coaching so he could see his sons play in college and in the NFL, he would have likely won more than 400 games and probably would have retired as the winningest head coach in state history. Even with the missing seasons, Johnson finished No. 3 on the all-time state list behind only Bob Ladoucuer of De La Salle (399) and Marijon Ancich of Santa Fe Springs St. Paul (366).

"Gosh no, I never coached for things like that," Bob Johnson said. "I had to do what's right. I could probably stay now. It's just in mid-season this year that it hit me that it was time. With those eight years, I would not have experienced things that I got to experience."

Johnson chose Mission Viejo as to where he'd restart his head coaching career, since the school was across the street from where he lives and where he had landed as a teacher after leaving El Toro.

"We had one tough year, then started rolling," he said of his career with the Diablos. "I've also been lucky in that I had good guys [assistant coaches] with me all the time."

One of those assistants at both El Toro and Mission Viejo was Marty Spaulding, who specialized in teaching and developing linemen. He wasn't coaching with Johnson for the last few seasons, but built a reputation as being one of the best line coaches in the nation.

Even though the team wasn't in the top division of the CIF Southern Section playoffs, Mission Viejo came on so strong under

Johnson that by 2004 the Diablos were contending for the No. 1 ranking in the state and nation. That team took on De La Salle of Concord that season and won 17–14 en route to a perfect regular season. That was the year that the Spartans had already lost twice before playing the Diablos, but it still was a signature win.

Mission Viejo then went on to finish 14–0 with a 49–21 triumph over Valencia for the CIF-SS Division 2 title. Among the other teams that the Diablos beat that season were both CIF-SS Division 1 finalists. The Diablos became the State Team of the Year and runner-up for the final national No. 1 ranking.

Quarterback Mark Sanchez, who later earned fame as the quarterback of the New York Jets, completed 63 percent of his passes for that 2004 team for 2,441 yards and 24 touchdowns. Junior fullback Chane "The Train" Moline, who later played at UCLA, rushed for 1,842 yards and scored 36 TDs. Future NFL player Nick Reed also played defensive end and junior tight end. Konrad Reuland was another standout. Reuland was on the Baltimore Ravens' practice squad in 2016 when he died at age twenty-nine from a brain aneurysm.

Following 2004, the Diablos continued to field teams consistently among the best in the state. They pushed their winning streak in 2005 to 41 games to set an Orange County record that still stands and went 12–1 in 2009, 13–1 in 2010, 11–1 in 2012, and 11–1 in 2013.

The 2015 season was the one the Johnsons had been waiting for, since that was when Brock, Bob's grandson and Bret's son, would be a senior. By that time, the CIF state bowl games were in full swing and even though the Diablos were unbeaten they weren't under serious consideration for the CIF Open Division since they weren't in the CIF-SS Pac-Five Division. It didn't matter though. Mission Viejo still had to play and beat strong competition to finish 16–0, including wins of 21–14 over Vista Murrieta, 32–28 over San Diego Section champ Helix, and then 24–0 over Bellarmine Prep of San Jose for the CIF Division 1-AA state crown.

Many who've followed the Johnsons for several years can remember when Brock was a ten-year-old running around the practice field with some of the nation's top college and high school quarterbacks during Elite 11 Quarterback Camps that his grandfather was directing and his dad was helping to coach. For those spectators, it was fun to see him years later pass for 3,607 yards with 41 touchdowns for that unbeaten, state title team. Brock broke another school record that his uncle or dad never got when he threw for seven touchdown passes in one game.

"He's just the most special kid and that's what made that season so great," Bob Johnson beamed. "Every teacher we've ever talked to all say that. He just has this empathy for all other kids. He's off the charts."

Brock spent one season at Georgetown after graduating from Mission Viejo, but left and was on the roster at UC Davis during the 2017 season. Bret and his wife Chalene, who have combined to build several multi-million-dollar life and fitness businesses, also have a daughter, Cierra, who in the spring of 2017 was one of the state's top 800-meter runners on the track.

Rob and his wife, Dana, have four children, and according to grandpa they all are in sports. "Rob was just here an hour ago picking up one of them and was going to another practice after that," Johnson said during an interview. Their daughters Tatum and Presley and sons Bo and Duke range in age from eleven to five, as of early in 2018.

Bob Johnson still gets sentimental about some of the other quarterbacks he has tutored over the years. In addition to his sons and Mark Sanchez, he also was a key figure in the development of longtime NFL quarterback Carson Palmer. Palmer didn't go to Mission Viejo but would always come to the Elite 11 camps when his former coach was directing those events in the late 2000s and early 2010s. Palmer, who also won a Heisman Trophy and was the No. 1 pick in the 2003 NFL Draft, recently retired from the NFL at age thirty-eight with 46,247 yards and 294 touchdowns. Based on those totals and on some of his other accomplishments, Palmer could someday be a member of the Pro Football Hall of Fame.

After his final game, when the Diablos lost to eventual CIF Open Division champion Mater Dei of Santa Ana 49–14 in the 2017 CIF-SS Division I semifinals, Bob caused a stir when he was quoted in the media that the Monarchs "were the best team money could buy."

One month later, as he was preparing for the final team banquet of his career, Johnson wasn't backing off that statement.

"I was referring to a system that isn't fair anymore. Mater Dei already has four transfers for next season [2018]. I know it's not just them. I'm glad I said it because I knew I was leaving. That's why I'm not coaching anymore. That's what stopped me. We were coaching knowing that our kids had no chance to win."

Maybe saying that wasn't the way some thought Johnson should end his coaching career. Despite his retirement though, there's still more to come from the Johnson family in terms of football. In fact, there could be more quarterbacks to watch and more quarterbacks who will coach, too.

18

Best and Most Unique Places to See a Game

The largest stadium to ever be used for a California high school football game is the Rose Bowl in Pasadena. From 1972 to 1997, the Rose Bowl had a seating capacity of 104,091. It went down to just over 90,000 after that.

In addition to hosting Super Bowls and college football National Championship Games, the Rose Bowl has been the site of games involving Pasadena high schools. The annual Turkey Tussle rivalry game between Pasadena High and Muir High of Pasadena was played for the 71st time in 2017 and the Rose Bowl was the site once again. Muir, which had running back and eventual baseball immortal Jackie Robinson on its football team in the 1930s, won the 2017 contest 33–21.

The smallest venue for a game possibly has been the front yard of a woman identified in newspaper articles in Inyo County in the 1970s as Mrs. Sorrell. Those were for 8-man matchups involving Death Valley High of Shoshone as the home school. People drove their cars to the makeshift field and parked off the side of the road. The school closed in 1990.

Perhaps ironically for such a large state, three of the most unique settings for high school football games are in San Francisco.

For stunning views of the Golden Gate Bridge and an enclosed sensation that is a must for any great place to watch a game, No. 1 might be George Washington High of San Francisco. Most games in the city, however, aren't played on Friday night and aren't heavily attended. Still, the national website MaxPreps once wrote that Washington's stadium is one of the 10 high school football stadiums in the nation to see before you die.

Galileo's George White Field doesn't have a view of the Golden Gate Bridge, but it's more historical, and if you can watch a game from one of the higher floors of the high-rise apartments across the street you'll get a view of the action that you've never seen before. Galileo coaches have been known to get permission from residents to film the action from there.

Galileo's stadium sits kitty-corner to the famed Ghirardelli Square near Fisherman's Wharf. The goal posts are so close to the street that balls from kicks have been known to ricochet off busses and cars and bang off the side of apartment buildings.

The Galileo venue used to be known as O. J. Simpson Field. The name was changed without fanfare after Simpson had been charged with the 1994 murders of his ex-wife, Nicole, and her friend, Ron Goldman. George White was a longtime coach of the team.

If one sits at the right spot at Galileo in October when it's Fleet Week in San Francisco, one could have a view of Alcatraz Island with the Blue Angels flying overhead as the Lions are battling one of their Academic Athletic Association rivals down below.

The other spot in San Francisco worth a visit is refurbished Kezar Stadium, which stands on the previous home stadium of the San Francisco 49ers. It used to seat 50,000 but was demolished and rebuilt to seat a much smaller crowd in 1989. The 49ers last played there in 1971. Kezar Stadium often hosts CIF San Francisco Section championship games these days as well as the rivalry game between St. Ignatius and Sacred Heart Cathedral. The SI-SHC rivalry is the oldest one west of the Mississippi River and dates back to 1892.

More top stadium choices would include Alex G. Spanos Stadium at Lincoln High School in Stockton, Balboa Stadium in San Diego (used mainly by San Diego High), Griffith Field at Bakersfield High in Bakersfield, Dunlavy Stadium at Sonora High in Sonora, and Valley Christian Field at Valley Christian High in San Jose.

Lincoln's stadium offers the prerequisite for many of the best football venues in that there is no running track that separates the fans from the teams, and therefore the fans are simply closer to the action. The stadium was improved several years ago by the addition of a college-like foyer entrance. Sycamore trees loom tall on one end of the field while the other side is enclosed by more grandstands. The press box at Lincoln also is one of the best anywhere, with more than one level.

A major reason Lincoln's stadium stands out is because it is located about two blocks from the longtime residence of San Diego Chargers majority owner Alex Spanos. The Spanos children—including Dean Spanos, the controlling owner and Chairman of the Board of the Chargers—are from Lincoln, and many grandchildren played inside the stadium. The Spanos family made such a stadium possible and deserve a lot of credit for their contributions not just to Stockton but to the entire state.

Balboa Stadium is similar to San Francisco's Kezar Stadium in that it once was the host site for a pro football team and it is part

The first-class stadium at Lincoln High in Stockton is named for San Diego Chargers' owner Alex Spanos, who has lived near the school for more than 50 years. *(Mark Tennis)*

of a larger park. For Kezar, it's Golden Gate Park. For Balboa, it's Balboa Park.

The Chargers played at Balboa Stadium from 1961 to 1966, but it was built many years before that. The original stadium, in fact, was built in 1914. San Diego High, which is nearby the stadium, and other schools from the San Diego Unified School District have used Balboa Stadium in recent years. The stadium once held 34,000 spectators, but after it was demolished in the 1970s it shrunk to 3,000.

Griffith Field is the home of Bakersfield High, which can be considered one of the two greatest high school football schools in California history (see Chapter One). From 2015 until early in the 2017 season, Griffith Field wasn't being used while undergoing a multi-million-dollar upgrade.

After everything was done, the same iconic traditions at Griffith Field were still there, including the locker rooms being underneath the grandstands and prominent granite blocks that give the place an almost menacing appearance to opposing teams. A water tower next to the field had to be removed, but a smaller one was put in its place just to add a touch of history to an already historical spot.

Dunlavy Stadium was built in 1937 when 5,500 seats were planted on the side of a hill surrounded by pine trees. Dunlavy often is mentioned as one of the most unique places to see a game. A fan can easily visit a restaurant or watering hole with a short walk to nearby downtown Sonora before or after a game.

It can be awkward when the fans of both teams sit on the same side of the steep grandstands, but Sonora's traditions as a Gold Rush town in Tuolumne County and its winning football teams combine to offer a memorable experience.

At Valley Christian, the parking can be notoriously awful, but the reason is because space is limited on the top of a hill that overlooks the sprawling Santa Clara Valley below. Fans who can park below and walk up the hill will slowly but surely take in a stunning landscape of hills, lights, and even planes on their approach to the San Jose airport. If it's sunset, the scenery is even more spectacular.

As a member of the famed West Catholic Athletic League, Valley Christian is guaranteed to have close, tense games at almost all home games.

19

A Very Strong Recruiting Analyst

Perhaps no aspect of California high school football has changed more in the last 10 to 15 years than the recruitment of players by colleges and the way in which that recruiting is covered by the media.

There's actually an entire media industry that follows the process of identifying top prospects when they're as young as the eighth grade, then evaluating those prospects as they get older and finally covering the often frantic final hours of Signing Day.

Before the 2017–18 season, Signing Day in early February was always the first time a graduating senior could sign a letter of intent, which served as a binding agreement between the athlete and school. Starting in 2017–18, players began to have the option of an earlier signing day in November. This seems beneficial for the ever-growing number of players who are graduating from their high schools after the first semester of their senior year so they can head to college faster, get into spring practices faster, and if dreams come true get to the NFL Draft faster.

There are several people in the Golden State who are entrenched in the world of football recruiting. One such expert is Brandon Huffman, the national director for 247Sports and Scout.com and a graduate of Ventura High. Huffman, who now lives in Washington, built his reputation in the field by following the top college prospects in California.

For Huffman, his passion for high school football and college football recruiting can be traced back to two games—one in which he played and one that he attended as a spectator when he was a senior in college.

At Ventura High in the mid-1990s, the Cougars were one of the top teams in the Ventura/Santa Barbara County region. This was before St. Bonaventure of Ventura and Oaks Christian of Westlake Village, two small private schools with deep pockets, began to build powerhouse programs.

"We had to overcome a lot because in the middle of my senior year our head coach [Harvey Kochel] was let go and replaced by Phil McCuen, the offensive coordinator," Huffman said by phone during a January of 2018 interview. "I was a 6-1, 225-pound tight end who mostly blocked for a team that ran the veer [offense]."

Despite the coaching change, Ventura had a chance to force a three-way tie for the Channel League title with a win at the end of Huffman's senior season against its crosstown arch-rivals from Buena High.

"Buena versus Ventura at that time was it," Huffman recalled. "There were nine to 10 thousand people that crammed into Larrabee Stadium and there were fans on both end zones. It was just so much fun.

"We never lost to Buena in our four years. We were kind of like a gritty little team that could just do what it took to beat them. I'll always remember that game. Here I am forty years old and all the details are still fresh."

Huffman indicated that there were two smaller colleges that showed some interest in him, but he decided to go to Azusa Pacific University in the San Gabriel Valley where he took the passion he had for the game and directed it more toward journalism and sports information. He worked for the student newspaper and did freelance stringing for *The San Gabriel Valley Tribune* and *The Whittier Daily News*.

In his senior year at Azusa Pacific, Huffman began to take more of an interest in players from outside the San Gabriel Valley. Justin Fargas from Notre Dame of Sherman Oaks and DeSean Foster of Tustin were two running backs at the time who were the talk of Southern California and who were getting scholarship offers from numerous major colleges. (Note: Remember Antonio Fargas, the actor who played Huggy Bear on the old *Starsky & Hutch* TV series? Justin Fargas is Antonio's son.)

As the CIF Southern Section playoffs got underway in 1997, Huffman and a friend were looking for a great matchup to attend. They found it in the Division V title game, which featured Foster (who later signed with UCLA) and his team from Tustin playing undefeated Santa Margarita of Rancho Santa Margarita, which had a talented quarterback named Carson Palmer.

"After watching those two go back-and-forth, I was hooked," Huffman remembered. "That also was just when the Internet was getting started."

Santa Margarita won that game 55–42 and the teams combined for more than 1,000 yards. Palmer, who would later win a Heisman Trophy at USC, passed for 413 yards and five touchdowns. Foster bolted for 378 yards on 32 carries and scored six times.

In 1998, just as Huffman was beginning his sportswriting career, Rivals.com was founded in the Seattle area by Jim Heckman, a son-in-law of former University of Washington head coach Don James. Huffman began writing for that site soon afterward. The initial business plan for Rivals.com was to try to get massive web traffic not just through content generated by college-based websites in a network but also via message boards where fans from different schools could banter back and forth. Ad revenue would then be collected based on that traffic.

As Rivals.com expanded, Huffman continued to provide recruiting updates on top California players. When the so-called "dot-com bubble" of late 2001 and early 2002 struck, however, Rivals.com briefly ceased operations. Several former executives of a company that Rivals.com had purchased, led by Shannon Terry and recruiting editor Bobby Burton, relaunched the network, but Heckman was no longer part of it. Heckman instead strived to build a different recruiting network of his own, calling it The Insiders, and Huffman started working there.

While doing work for The Insiders in 2003, Huffman was approached by Tracy Pierson, who was running that network's UCLA site, and was asked to provide content not just for him but for WeAreSC.com, the network's USC site. A few months later, Huffman became the primary California recruiting source at The Insiders.

In 2005, The Insiders was renamed Scout.com and was sold for a reported $60 million to Fox Interactive. Huffman was Scout's California/West Region editor and he's been moving up in that company ever since. Huffman was assigned to a manager's role in 2007, became a national manager in 2011, and in 2014 was named the recruiting editor of the Scout network.

"In the beginning, I would just call local recruits and find out what they were doing," said Huffman, who is often quoted by local media throughout the country about certain recruits, which colleges did the best each year, and how NCAA rules changes may impact the recruiting landscape. "We'd get on a schedule and call a kid maybe once per month. Now, a kid tweets and might tweet five times in one day that he has gotten offers."

It's that explosion of social media that has vastly disrupted the way Huffman and other well-known recruiting analysts, such as Greg Biggins (also of Scout.com and a former colleague when Cal-Hi Sports was part of Student Sports), cover college football recruiting. Another huge change has been the rise of Hudl. com in recent years. Hudl.com is a site and application that helps coaches and players with game film. Not that long ago, Huffman can tell you, he'd be sent package after package of video tape in the mail.

"That's what a good prospect would have to do," he said. "With Hudl, everybody has a highlight film. Everybody can be seen on film. No longer are there guys who are obscure as recruits because of not having film."

Still, despite the availability of film, despite Huffman knowing about more and more eighth graders through AAU-style 7-on-7 passing tournaments, and despite even more combines and events designed to highlight top prospects, there are players that someday will be in the NFL who were not covered very much if at all by the recruiting media.

A great example of that is Julian Edelman of the New England Patriots. He was injured during the 2017 season, but in 2016 he was one of the Patriots' top players and came up with several game-changing plays in Super Bowl LI to help New England beat the Atlanta Falcons 34–28 after it was behind 28–3 in the third quarter.

Edelman wasn't a blip on any recruiting editor's notebook during his senior year (2004) at Woodside High in the San Francisco Bay Area. He did help Woodside go 13–0 and he passed for more than 2,000 yards in two seasons, but he didn't have the size to be a college quarterback. After not signing on Letter of Intent Day, Edelman went to College of San Mateo, where he continued to be a jack-of-all-trades type of quarterback. He played well enough there so that Kent State University offered him a scholarship. Yet it wasn't until after Edelman was drafted in the seventh round in 2009 by the Patriots and then began to become a slot receiver that his football career really took off.

"We're wrong sometimes, but NFL offices can be wrong too," Huffman said. "You would have thought that after Aaron Rodgers [who attended Pleasant Valley High in Chico, then Butte College, and then finally Cal] that it wouldn't happen again, but it does. Even now, guys fall through the cracks. There also are a lot of [college] coaches that take the easy way out. They might recruit a kid who's a backup at a school like St. John Bosco [Bellflower] because of a recommendation instead of working harder to find that guy from a school in the Central Valley.

"When [head coach] Chris Petersen was at Boise State, he would find them all the time. A player like Doug Martin [from

St. Mary's of Stockton]—the big schools didn't spend time on him. Petersen got him, and Martin became a first-round [NFL] pick. There are some really good coaches who are still doing that."

On the other side of the spectrum, there are those physically mature high school juniors and seniors who just ooze so much size, speed, and skill that any recruiting analyst or any prep sportswriter with even a few years of experience can just tell what the future may hold.

"I love to tell the story of Tyron Smith [Dallas Cowboys], who is now one of the best linemen in the NFL," Huffman began. "He came to a Nike camp at USC and looked like a man against boys. We knew beforehand of just his name and that he played for [head coach] Pete Duffy [at Rancho Verde of Moreno Valley].

"And at the end of their junior seasons, we had JuJu Smith [now JuJu Smith-Schuster of the Pittsburgh Steelers] and Adoree Jackson [played in 2017 for the Tennessee Titans] as the No. 1 and No. 2 players in their class. I call those guys 'no doubters' because there's no doubt to me that after high school they'll be in the NFL in three years."

Many in Northern California felt the same way in 2015 and 2016 watching Najee Harris play as a running back at Antioch. Harris was the 2015 Mr. Football State Player of the Year as a junior and an All-American as a senior. As a true freshman at Alabama in 2017, he finished the season with a team-leading 64 yards rushing on a handful of carries when the Crimson Tide defeated Georgia in the College Football Playoff National Championship.

Avery Strong

As Huffman was continuing to work as a national editor for Scout. com in 2015 and to build his family with his wife, Amanda, his world was rocked. What began with a visit to an ophthalmologist

Brandon Huffman is one of the most successful recruiting reporters and editors in the nation, but in 2015 and 2016 had to experience the diagnosis, illness, and death of his daughter Avery from a rare form of cancer. *(Courtesy Huffman family)*

with their five-year-old daughter, Avery, about double vision in one eye ended with a devastating diagnosis: their little girl had diffuse intrinsic pontine glioma, a rare form of brain cancer that is inoperable.

Despite the dire circumstances and the fact that Avery was still a young child, she displayed remarkable courage and inspired many players that her father was covering. A social media movement known as #AveryStrong gathered thousands of supporters from around the nation and even from around the world. The media coverage by outlets ranging from *USA Today*, to the *Washington Post, Entertainment Weekly*, FOX, NBC, CBS, and *Sports Illustrated* helped spread the word of her story as well.

Avery underwent several series of radiation treatments that began in the summer of 2015 under the direction of Mary Bridge Children's Hospital in Tacoma. She attended first grade classes as much as possible and strived to enjoy as many of the normal activities that she liked before she got sick.

Avery Hayden Huffman died on February 16, 2016, with Brandon, Amanda, and their other three children—Alexandra, fourteen (in 2018); Kade, twelve; and Addison, six—surrounding her.

"It will always be hard for us during the holidays and then out to the middle of February when she died," Huffman reflected. "We started the foundation to turn our grief into something positive."

The official name of the foundation is the Avery Huffman Defeat DIPG Foundation, but the web address is averystrongdipg.org.

20

The Most Unforgettable Coach

People frequently refer to their spouse or longtime companion as a "soulmate." For an outsider to sense that connection between two people may seem impossible, but not to anyone who ever spent time around former Los Gatos High football coach Charlie Wedemeyer and his wife, Lucy, especially when Charlie—who started there in 1977—was still head coach of the Wildcats in 1984 and 1985 as the effects of his battle with Lou Gehrig's disease were taking a huge toll on him.

In those two seasons, Wedemeyer nearly died from the disease's various afflictions. But he continued to attend every game, called every offensive play, and devised every game plan. Charlie could do it all, because Lucy was always there for him. With Charlie unable to walk or even talk in 1985, Lucy drove him along the sidelines at games in a golf cart. She was the one who could read his lips, knew every twitch of his eyes and mouth, and relayed which plays Charlie wanted to call. She was the one who took care of their kids and arranged for Charlie's around-the-clock nursing needs.

For 34 years, dating to when Charlie was first feeling the effects of the disease in 1977, until he died at age sixty-four in 2010, Lucy was by his side. The two met when they were both students at Punahou High in Honolulu, where Charlie was a football star. Charlie was following the path of older brother Herman "Squirmin" Wedemeyer, who later became an All-American running back at St. Mary's College in Moraga and an actor on the *Hawaii Five-O* TV series.

"He was very humble and never wanted to be in the spotlight," Lucy recalled of their high school years during a February 2017 interview. "I found that very refreshing for an athlete of that category. He was a big deal."

After Charlie and Lucy graduated from Punahou, a school that later gained fame as being where President Barack Obama came from, they stayed together when Charlie went off to play college football at Michigan State. They were married by his sophomore year. As a freshman, he was on the MSU team in 1966 that tied Notre Dame in the "Game of the Century" but still had a claim on the national title.

The young couple had happier years together before the diagnosis. After he was done playing football and got his master's degree, Charlie took a job at Los Gatos High in the San Francisco Bay Area as a teacher and football coach. Charlie and Lucy welcomed a daughter, Carri, in 1967, during Lucy's sophomore year of college after they got married. Their son, Kale, was born in 1970.

There is no cure for Amyotrophic lateral sclerosis, which is the technical name of Lou Gehrig's disease. When someone gets it, the motor skills in the hands, feet, and legs deteriorate first. Walking then gets difficult, usually requiring the patient to be wheelchair-bound. Eventually, talking and breathing become troublesome and 24-hour nursing care is the norm. According

Charlie and Lucy Wedemeyer are shown in the early 1980s with Los Gatos football players before Charlie's disease caused him to breathe through a tube. *(Courtesy Wedemeyer Family)*

to the ALS Association, the average life expectancy for someone who is diagnosed with ALS is two to five years.

"At the beginning, it was always 'We are a team and this is our disease,'" Lucy said. "Our faith is what drove us to keep going."

Charlie lived such a long time with it because he could breathe through an air hose attached after a tracheotomy, he could be fed through a tube in his stomach, and he had something and someone to live for. It was football in those early years, then it became inspiring others with his story both for Christian audiences (he was a man of great faith) and non-Christians. He was honored at a national convention for ALS in 2002 along with Major League Baseball Hall of Famer Cal Ripken Jr.

The cruelest aspect of Lou Gehrig's disease might be that while the body's nervous system gets attacked, the brain doesn't. A great example of that is world-renowned physicist Dr. Stephen Hawking of England. Despite his more than 40-year battle with ALS, Dr. Hawking has changed the world with his theories.

"I first met Charlie and Lucy when I visited Berkeley in 1988 and they struck me as very positive and very determined not to let ALS defeat them," Dr. Hawking said through a computer voice during an interview for a documentary about Charlie first shown on PBS in 2009. "Charlie and I have problems but so do other people. Nearly everyone has some difficulty in their life. The trick is not to complain but to get out and meet the challenge as well as one can. I guess Charlie and I came to the same conclusion."

In the same documentary, Lucy read Charlie's lips for a response to what Dr. Hawking had stated.

"Sometime in our lives we are all faced with some type of adversity that may be tough to deal with, but when the time comes you have to make a choice," Charlie said. "We can choose to feel sorry for ourselves and be miserable and cause everyone around to be miserable or choose, with God's help, to go through it knowing that we will come out of it better and stronger. To borrow a phrase from a friend of ours, Tim Hansel, pain and suffering are inevitable but misery is optional. We make the choice."

Switching Roles

Horace "Butch" Cattolico was in his fifth year at Fox Lane High School in New York as a varsity football assistant coach in the 1975–76 school year when he and his wife, Berit, decided to head back to California. Butch had grown up in the Bay Area and was a football standout at Pittsburg High in Contra Costa County. He went to the University of California-Berkeley and was on the football team, although he says, "I mostly sat on the bench."

Upon his return to the Bay Area, Butch accepted a job as a math teacher and assistant football coach in Los Gatos.

During the 1976 football season, he worked alongside another coach who was fairly new to the school, Charlie Wedemeyer. Neither of them knew what was in store over the course of the next eight seasons.

"It started with his hands," Cattolico said in a February 2017 phone interview that was conducted one day after his 69th birthday. "He'd complain that his hands don't work. Then he told us he fell a couple of times.

"Before the 1978 season, Frank Griffin, who was our team doctor, sat us all down and told us that Charlie had gotten Lou Gehrig's disease. Most of us didn't know about it and Charlie didn't accept it and wouldn't believe it."

Wedemeyer was the Wildcats' head coach when he received the diagnosis. He certainly wasn't going to step down despite the dire circumstances and his assistants weren't going anywhere, either.

"I talked to the principal and told him as long as Charlie can be the head coach I would be glad to work for him," Cattolico commented.

For the next few seasons, Wedemeyer continued to build the Los Gatos program while battling the disease. The 1980 team finished second in the West Valley Athletic League with a 7–4 record. The 1982 team won the WVAL crown but lost in the first round of the CCS playoffs 21–14 to Los Altos. Then in 1983 the Wildcats won the WVAL title again and they were unbeaten in the regular season (9–0) entering the playoffs. They were upset that year, however, 18–14 by St. Ignatius of San Francisco.

By that time, everyone in the CCS coaching community knew what Wedemeyer, his staff, and his family was going through. His coaching had to be done with the golf cart by then and his speaking voice was down to a whisper.

"We were all chosen to work for a high school all-star game in the summer of 1984 and that's when Charlie got real sick," Cattolico recalled. "I was actually working with our players [at Los Gatos] while Charlie and two other assistant coaches, Bill Burnham and Eric Van Patton, were doing the all-stars. There was this big fire in Los Gatos and Charlie couldn't handle the smoke."

Wedemeyer was forced to go to the hospital. His condition was serious, but he was determined to coach in the all-star game and called plays from his phone at the hospital. That all-star game is now called the Charlie Wedemeyer All-Star Football Game and was played for the 44th time in July of 2018 at Levi's Stadium in Santa Clara.

"He probably almost died that summer," Cattolico said. "That's when we had to make a decision. That's when he had the tracheotomy. He didn't know how to walk anymore and now he had lost the ability to talk."

Wedemeyer's teaching days were over several years earlier, but he still wanted to coach. He still yearned to be the head coach. It was getting more difficult for Cattolico to travel back and forth to spend the extra time with Charlie at his home, still serve as assistant coach, teach four classes per day, and devote time to his own growing family, but he knew the 1984 season might be special.

"That's also when Lucy came even more on board," Cattolico remembered. "We worked out a system so she could get the plays from him and give them to me. Football does have a pretty select vocabulary so she didn't have to know that many words. There were signals and sounds and we were able to make it work.

"The hardest part for all of it was that Charlie's mind never left. He was focused and creative in what he wanted to do."

Most offensive coordinators who call plays in football games these days are up in the press box wearing headsets. Charlie was sitting in a golf cart with a breathing tube attached to his throat.

"We had to feed him a lot of info as the games were going on and it was hard sometimes for him to see what he wanted to see," Cattolico said. "We were always trying to clear a path in front of the cart and to the sides so he could see the field as much as possible."

Lucy said she would frequently have to move the cart two inches at a time, back up six inches here and six inches there.

"We were so afraid someone was going to run into us," she added. "And the funny thing about driving the cart is that Charlie was the one who taught me how to drive [back in Hawaii]."

The reading of Charlie's lips and then giving the plays to Cattolico or the quarterback are what most people think of with regard to the Wedemeyer coaching story. But what about all of the days leading up to the game and practicing in August?

At home, Lucy said a video playback system was set up so Charlie could watch the film. At the time, he could move his foot and tap the buttons on the VCR. "The biggest thing was how many times he'd rewind. He loved it."

Even before the diagnosis, Wedemeyer had a nickname as the "Hawaiian Eye" for his knack of finding characteristics in opposing players and for being able to see out of the corner of his eye.

With the best collection of athletes that Wedemeyer and Cattolico had ever had in their years together at Los Gatos, the 1984 team was dominating as expected. Unfortunately, the Wildcats were upset in the CCS semifinals 15–14 by St. Francis of Mountain View.

The arrangement of Lucy relaying the plays through Charlie's lips continued in 1985 with a different result. Los Gatos flipped the script with an upset of St. Francis in the CCS championship game. It also was the last game Charlie was the school's head coach.

"I just told the principal [Ted Simonson] after that year that Charlie could stay as the head coach but that I might need to leave," Cattolico recalled. "It was hard. I was spending hours and hours at his house, we had kids by then, and I was doing four math classes per day. I didn't want to leave but needed something to change."

In the spring, the school's administration decided it would make a change. Simonson told Cattolico that he wanted him to be the head coach. Simonson also told the *San Jose Mercury-News* that he didn't want to lose Cattolico as a math teacher. After that, Cattolico went to Wedemeyer and talked. They knew Charlie wanted to continue to coach, so they in effect switched roles. Charlie would now be an assistant on Cattolico's staff. He didn't call plays, but worked with quarterbacks and running backs and helped on game management.

The Wildcats didn't exactly suffer with Cattolico as head coach. He was comfortable with the school, he continued to teach all math subjects, and he took the foundation of what Charlie started and won 11 more CCS titles plus 16 more league championships until he retired in 2012.

The pinnacle of Cattolico's years as head coach came in the early 2000s, when he began working with Trent Edwards, a quarterback with major college potential. Los Gatos was 13–0 with a CCS title in the 2000 season and was No. 3 in the final Cal-Hi Sports Division II state rankings. In 2001, the Wildcats repeated all of those accomplishments and were chosen the Division III State Team of the Year.

Edwards passed for more than 2,000 yards in both seasons, but gained the most recognition for completing a high percentage of his passes. As a junior, he set a state record completing 78.1 percent of his throws and after his senior year Edwards had a state record with a 74.8 percent total for his three-year career.

Los Gatos continued to win in the 2002 season and eventually put together a streak of 38 victories in a row, which is still the second longest winning streak in CCS history.

When Cattolico retired in 2012 with 264 wins, the only coach in CCS history with more career wins than him was Saratoga's Benny Pierce, who had 270 from 1961 to 1994. San Jose Bellarmine's Mike Janda eclipsed Pierce's record in 2016.

Other players that Cattolico coached at Los Gatos in addition to Charlie's son Kale—the team's top player in the late '80s who later played at Cal—and Edwards (who later played at Stanford and four years in the NFL) were linebacker Kiko Alonso (who played his sixth season in the NFL in 2017) and defensive end Jared Allen (who was one of the top pass rushers in the NFL for many years).

It soon became clear that Cattolico's football prowess ran in the family, with regard to his son Joe.

In fact, it didn't take long after Joe graduated from Princeton to find that his career of choice would be exactly the same as his father's. By age twenty-two, Joe was already coaching and in his mid-20s was leading teams to championships at Overfelt High of San Jose and then later at Independence High of San Jose.

"Those years were fun because we were running the same offense and defense and we'd scrimmage before the season started," Cattolico stated. "And in the off-season, we'd find a clinic we both liked, jumped on a plane, and tried to learn as much as we could."

In 2012, after Butch retired at Los Gatos, there was speculation that Joe—then at Pleasant Grove High of Elk Grove—might take over his father's job. Instead, it was Butch and Berit who moved. They bought a house three doors down from Joe and his growing family.

For the 2013 season, Butch was coaching again, but this time it would be as an assistant helping out his son's team. Joe left Pleasant Grove after the 2013 season, took an 18-month hiatus from coaching, and in 2015 took over a struggling program at Sheldon High of Sacramento, which also is in the Elk Grove Unified School District. The Huskies went from two wins to eight in Joe's first season. Butch coached on the staff with Joe during the 2015, 2016, and 2017 seasons.

The 1984–85 Seasons

Attending the 1984 CIF Central Coast Section Division I semi-finals was about as difficult an assignment for any journalist to complete. Most in the local Bay Area prep sports community were aware of Charlie Wedemeyer's illness. As the Wildcats kept winning, the real possibility of them going unbeaten and winning a section title in the midst of it all was tantalizing.

As they say, there is no rooting in the press box. But someone would have had to have been a robot not to root for Charlie's team to win.

Los Gatos had never won a CCS title entering the 1984 season and had lost several times in the playoffs to teams with lesser win-loss records. That all contributed to a semifinal matchup against 8–2–1 St. Francis of Mountain View as a daunting task for Wedemeyer and his players even though they were 11–0. St. Francis in those years was known for its playoff success, including having the Cal-Hi Sports State Team of the Year one season earlier.

"The '84 team probably was the best group of athletes Los Gatos has ever had," said Cattolico about a squad that averaged 40 points per game running Charlie's offense. "We had teams that were better, but that one was exceptional talent-wise."

The game against St. Francis was played at Independence in inclement weather. Both teams struggled to move the ball, but the conditions favored the Lancers, who were more comfortable playing a slugfest in the slop due to their participation in a rough-and-tumble league.

"There was four inches of mud and that made it harder for Charlie in the cart as well," Cattolico remembered. "The game went into overtime and in those days we used the old tie-breaker in which the ball is placed at the 50-yard line."

Under those tie-breaker rules, each team runs four plays and the team with the ball on the other squad's side of the field after those plays gets one point and the win. The Wildcats were handed a holding penalty on their second play, which they couldn't overcome. St. Francis got a 15–14 victory and Los Gatos was done at 11–1.

Fans and players on the Los Gatos sidelines were more despondent than what is usually the case in those circumstances. They knew how hard it was for Charlie and Lucy and the other coaches. This might be it. Charlie might not make it for another season, and an awful lot of seniors were graduating.

"It was a bad call," Lucy quickly blurted out when asked about the 1984 game. "We were told a few weeks later that the officials had made a mistake. I just remember telling Charlie, 'God has a plan.'"

The phrase "one more" also was already being uttered frequently by other coaches and players at Los Gatos. Charlie always told the kids "one more" when they were doing drills and practicing plays. Two film producers working on a documentary about Wedemeyer told him that "you've got to have one more season," according to Lucy.

It all worked because Cattolico and the other coaches all returned for the 1985 season and Charlie was ready, too. If anything, he looked thicker, his face fuller. The Wildcats weren't the favorites, with many new players who came up from the junior varsity and with seniors who were backups from the previous season. But they had something else.

It was a good sign for Los Gatos in the first round of the 1985 CCS playoffs. The team faced Bellarmine Prep of San Jose, and the result was a 19–0 shutout. The Wildcats then took on Santa Clara Valley Athletic League champ Los Altos and prevailed 27–15.

In the semifinals, Los Gatos faced Gilroy. This time, the Wildcats posted a 14–10 win. Even though they had improved their record to 11–1, they knew what was facing them in the championship game: St. Francis.

The Lancers were always a threat in those years under head coach Ron Calcagno and have continued to be into the late 2010s under head coach Greg Calcagno, Ron's son. They were the two-time defending champions in 1985 and were unbeaten at 12–0 with a top-five state ranking.

After the Los Gatos team had completed its warmups, Lucy drove the cart with Charlie down the ramp at Spartan Stadium for the CCS championship.

"It was so surreal just to be there because it was rainy and cold and there we were," Lucy said. "Charlie was just saying to me how thankful he was that he got to be here."

Like the 1984 game in the mud, the Los Gatos defense kept the Wildcats close. Jeff Borgese found some running room on offense and was able to punch in a pair of touchdowns. The special teams came through by converting two extra points.

As the game clock was running down, St. Francis was trailing 14–12, but had the ball and was marching down the field. Calcagno had trust in his players. He only needed a field goal and his team would have a fourth straight section title. Los Gatos and Wedemeyer would be crushed again.

With 42 seconds left, the Lancers set up for a 29-yard field goal attempt that probably would have won the game. A swarm of Wildcats, however, blocked the kick. The game was over and according to sportswriter Merv Harris of the *San Francisco Examiner*, the attention of everyone at Spartan Stadium shifted immediately to the golf cart.

"There wasn't a dry eye in the house," he said later to another writer who decided to go to a different section championship game on the same night.

After the celebrating had quieted, the process of placing Charlie into the specialized van had begun. The St. Francis bus was nearby and noticed what was happening. The bus stopped and the players and coaches began popping out of the front door.

"Every one of those kids [from St. Francis] came over and hugged Charlie," Lucy remembered. "They kept saying if they had to lose that they were glad it was to him."

Less than a month later, Wedemeyer was named State Coach of the Year and in the announcement for that honor it was stressed that he would have gotten it even if he was walking along the sidelines and yelling encouragement to his players. His final coaching record was 78–18–1 with one section title and seven league titles.

"It's a good thing we were all young when that happened," Cattolico said. "I don't know if it could happen that way today. But Charlie was an amazing guy. Everybody liked him and he was very intelligent. We all wanted to help as much as we could. And Lucy spending all those hours and hours with him, getting him ready, was truly incredible. Somehow, it just all came to fruition on that night."

Charlie's courage and Lucy's loving support wasn't just well known in California. In their home state of Hawaii, the headline above the fold on the front page of the *Honolulu Star-Bulletin* the day after Charlie died in 2010 declared: "Aloha, Charlie."

Companion Lists
for Various Chapters

Note: These are presented in the order of each chapter. All are based on reported information to the Cal-Hi Sports state record files through the 2017 season (including playoffs). Some of the chapters have no accompanying list. Some have more than one. For the chapter on California quarterbacks, there were lists compiled exclusively for this book of the state's Top 20 Greatest Players from all other positions. For longer lists, state record updates, and more information on many of the players, teams, and schools, visit CalHiSports.com.

HIGH SCHOOL FOOTBALL IN CALIFORNIA

Top 15 Winningest Schools in California High School Football

(Using rugby as a substitute for football during early 20th century)

780—Bakersfield, 1896–1942, 1945–2017 (780–268–43)*

767—Long Beach Poly, 1904–2017*

661—Berkeley, 1891–2017 (661–423–61)**

649—Los Angeles Loyola, 1908–1909, 1913–1917, 1919–2017 (649–306–37)

647—Santa Monica, 1898–2017 (647–398–51)***

646—Palo Alto, 1897–2016

642—San Jose Bellarmine, 1897–2017

639—Dos Palos, 1923–2017 (639–274–25)

628—Eureka, 1901–2017

621—Santa Barbara, 1900–1905, 1908–2017 (621–411–33)

618—Pittsburg, 1924–2017 (618–290–40)

601—Santa Ana, 1894–2017 (601–518–45)

593—Tehachapi, 1930–2017 (593–310–25)

589—Los Angeles, 1893–2017 (589–430–73) (forfeit losses in 2010, 2013, 2016 not included)

586—Vallejo, 1898–1900, 1907–1914, 1922–2017

582—Lompoc, 1921–2017 (582–356–21)

581—San Francisco Lowell, 1891–2017 (incomplete before 1923; forfeit win in 2009 not included)

*Bakersfield total doesn't include 22 wins and three losses by default; seven of the wins forfeited in 1984. Long Beach Poly total doesn't include four forfeit losses from 2015.

**Plus six wins and two losses by default; record also incomplete for 1890s.

***Plus six wins and one loss by default.

Top 25 Greatest Teams in California Football History

(Note: These are updated after every season and teams can move up and down based on the success of players on these teams after high school)

1. De La Salle (Concord) 2001
Record: 12–0; Head Coach: Bob Ladouceur

2. Vallejo 1954
Record: 9–0; Head Coach: Bob Patterson

3. Long Beach Poly 1959
Record: 11–0; Head Coach: Dave Levy

4. De La Salle (Concord) 1998
Record: 12–0; Head Coach: Bob Ladouceur

5. Eisenhower (Rialto) 1993
Record: 14–0; Head Coach: Tom Hoak

6. Bellarmine Prep (San Jose) 1965
Record: 9–0; Head Coach: John Hanna

7. De La Salle (Concord) 2003
Record: 13–0; Head Coach: Bob Ladouceur

8. Carson 1971
Record: 12–0; Head Coach: Gene Vollnogle

9. Long Beach Poly 2001
Record: 13–1; Head Coach: Raul Lara

10. Blair (Pasadena) 1969
Record: 13–0; Head Coach: Pete Yoder

11. Mater Dei (Santa Ana) 2017
Record: 15–0; Head Coach: Bruce Rollinson

12. St. John Bosco (Bellflower) 2013
Record: 16–0; Head Coach: Jason Negro

13. Mission Viejo 2004
Record: 14–0; Head Coach: Bob Johnson

14. De La Salle (Concord) 1994
Record: 13–0; Head Coach: Bob Ladouceur

15. Centennial (Corona) 2008
Record: 15–0; Head Coach: Matt Logan

16. Cordova (Rancho Cordova) 1975
Record: 11–0; Head Coach: Dewey Guerra

17. De La Salle (Concord) 1999
Record: 12–0; Head Coach: Bob Ladouceur

HIGH SCHOOL FOOTBALL IN CALIFORNIA

18. Mater Dei (Santa Ana) 1994
Record: 14–0; Head Coach: Bruce Rollinson

19. De La Salle (Concord) 2014
Record: 14–0; Head Coach: Justin Alumbaugh

20. Folsom 2014
Record: 16–0; Head Coach: Kris Richardson

21. Fontana 1987
Record: 14–0; Head Coach: Dick Bruich

22. De La Salle (Concord) 2010
Record: 15–0; Head Coach: Bob Ladouceur

23. El Rancho (Pico Rivera) 1966
Record: 12–0; Head Coach: Ernie Johnson

24. Bakersfield 1927
Record: 12–0; Head Coach: Dwight "Goldie" Griffith

25. El Toro (Lake Forest) 1986
Record: 14–0; Head Coach: Bob Johnson

2017 CIF State Champions

Open Division: Mater Dei (Santa Ana)
Division 1-AA: Folsom
Division 1-A: Narbonne (Harbor City)
Division 2-AA: Serra (San Mateo)
Division 2-A: St. Francis (Mountain View)
Division 3-AA: Bishop Diego (Santa Barbara)
Division 3-A: Steele Canyon (Spring Valley)
Division 4-AA: Crenshaw (Los Angeles)
Division 4-A: Milpitas
Division 5-AA: McClymonds (Oakland)
Division 5-A: Fortuna
Division 6-AA: Strathmore
Division 6-A: Galileo (San Francisco)

Updated State Record Lists
After 2017 Season

(Individual Passing & Scoring)

Most Yards Passing (Season)

* Note: all players in the subsequent sections were seniors, unless otherwise noted.

5,737—Jake Browning, Folsom, 2013 (15) Jr.

5,704—Jake Browning, Folsom, 2014 (16)

5,338—Tristan Gebbia, Calabasas, 2016 (15)

5,248—Jake Browning, Folsom, 2012 (15) Soph.

5,185—Tanner Trosin, Folsom, 2011 (14)

5,139—Jayden Daniels, San Bernardino Cajon, 2017 (16) Jr.

4,919—Noah Davis, Eureka St. Bernard's, 2014 (13)

4,907—David Koral, Pacific Palisades, 1999 (13) Jr.

4,899—Anthony Gordon, Pacifica Terra Nova, 2014 (13)

4,849—JT Daniels, Santa Ana Mater Dei, 2016 (14) Soph.

4,838—Kyle Boller, Newhall Hart, 1998 (14)

4,535—Brady White, Newhall Hart, 2013 (15) Jr.

Most Touchdown Passes (Season)

91—Jake Browning, Folsom, 2014 (15)

75—Jake Browning, Folsom, 2013 (15) Jr.

67—JT Daniels, Santa Ana Mater Dei, 2016 (14) Jr.

63—Robert De La Cruz, Los Angeles Cathedral, 1999 (13)

63—Jake Browning, Folsom, 2012 (15) Soph.

62—Dano Graves, Folsom, 2010 (15)

62—Jayden Daniels, San Bernardino Cajon, 2017 (16) Jr.

61—Robert De La Cruz, Los Angeles Cathedral, 1998 (13) Jr.

61—Tristan Gebbia, Calabasas, 2016 (15)

59—Kyle Boller, Newhall Hart, 1998 (14)

57—Jimmy Clausen, Westlake Village Oaks Christian, 2004 (14) Soph.

57—Jorge Hernandez, Torrance North, 2012 (14)

57—Kaiden Bennett, Folsom, 2017 (16) Jr.

HIGH SCHOOL FOOTBALL IN CALIFORNIA

57—T. J. Campbell, Eureka St. Bernard's, 2017 (12)
56—David Koral, Pacific Palisades, 1999 (13) Jr.
56—Caden Voges, Sacramento, 2014 (13) Jr.
55—Mitch Daniels, Concord, 2014 (13)

Most Yards Passing (Career)

16,775—Jake Browning, Folsom, 2012–2014 (45)
13,109—Tristan Gebbia, Calabasas, 2014–2016
12,014—JT Daniels, Santa Ana Mater Dei, 2015–2017 (41)
11,913—Sam Metcalf, Farmersville, 2011–2014
11,510—Caden Voges, Sacramento, 2013–2015
11,386—Braxton Burmeister, La Jolla Country Day, 2013–2016
11,397—Armando Herrera, Redlands East Valley, 2013–2016
11,022—Michael Herrick, Valencia, 2003–2005 (36)
10,835—Brady White, Newhall Hart, 2012–2014
10,677—Jimmy Clausen, Westlake Village Oaks Christian, 2003–2006 (53)

Most Touchdown Passes (Career)

229—Jake Browning, Folsom, 2012–2014 (45)
152—JT Daniels, Santa Ana Mater Dei, 2015–2017 (41)
145—Jimmy Clausen, Westlake Village Oaks Christian, 2003–2006 (53)
142—Caden Voges, Sacramento, 2013–2015
141—Tristan Gebbia, Calabasas, 2014–2016
140—Sam Metcalf, Farmersville, 2011–2014
132—Robert De La Cruz, Los Angeles Cathedral, 1997–1999
127—Braxton Burmeister, La Jolla Country Day, 2013–2016
117—Andrew Tovar, Los Angeles Cathedral, 2013–2016
117—Armando Herrera, Redlands East Valley, 2013–2016

Most Touchdowns Scored (Season)

72—Kazmeir Allen, Tulare, 2017 (15)
64—Tyler Ebell, Ventura, 2000 (14)
59—DeShaun Foster, Tustin, 1997 (14)
57—Jermaine Marshall, Malibu Camp Kilpatrick, 1999 (14)
57—Jake Taylor, Lake Arrowhead Rim of the World, 2012 (14)

57—Edgar Segura, Mendota, 2013 (13)

56—Tyler Gaffney, San Diego Cathedral Catholic, 2008 (14)

56—Sty Hairston, Banning, 2012 (13)

56—Eric Melesio, Riverside Norte Vista, 2016 (14)

Most Rushing Yards (Season)

4,495—Tyler Ebell, Ventura, 2000 (14)

4,459—Eric Melesio, Riverside Norte Vista, 2016 (14)

4,036—Jake Taylor, Lake Arrowhead Rim of the World, 2012 (14)

3,734—Tre Watson, Corona Centennial, 2013 (15)

3,586—Jermaine Marshall, Malibu Camp Kilpatrick, 1999 (14)

3,523—David Dotson, Moreno Valley View, 1991 (11)

3,488—Olito Thompson, Concord, 2011 (14) Jr.

3,460—Edgar Segura, Mendota, 2013 (13)

3,437—Chad Kackert, Simi Valley Grace Brethren, 2004 (12)

3,416—John Bordenkircher, Dixon, 1997 (12)

3,398—DeShaun Foster, Tustin, 1997 (14)

3,396—Ryan Mathews, Bakersfield West, 2006 (12)

3,376—Sty Hairston, Banning, 2012 (13)

3,336—Kazmeir Allen, Tulare Union, 2017 (14)

3,266—Tiquan Gilmore, Los Angeles Torres, 2016 (12) Jr.

Most Yards Total Offense (Season)

9,047—Corona Centennial, 2013 (15)

8,632—Folsom, 2014 (16)

8,570—Corona Centennial, 2012 (16)

8,072—San Bernardino Cajon, 2017 (16)

7,985—Corona Centennial, 2010 (15)

7,932—Folsom, 2016 (16)

7,913—Murrieta Murrieta Valley, 2016 (14)

7,818—Folsom, 2013 (15)

7,778—Stockton St. Mary's, 2016 (16)

7,699—Corona Centennial, 2015 (15)

HIGH SCHOOL FOOTBALL IN CALIFORNIA

All-Time Greatest Top 20 Players from California High Schools

(Based on NFL & college accomplishments and not on what each player did during high school)

Quarterbacks

1. Tom Brady (Serra, San Mateo)
2. John Elway (Granada Hills)
3. Aaron Rodgers (Pleasant Valley, Chico)
4. Dan Fouts (St. Ignatius, San Francisco)
5. Warren Moon (Hamilton, Los Angeles)
6. Jim Plunkett (James Lick, San Jose)
7. Carson Palmer (Santa Margarita, Rancho SM)
8. Norm Van Brocklin (Acalanes, Lafayette)
9. Bob Waterfield (Van Nuys)
10. John Brodie (Oakland Tech)
11. Randall Cunningham (Santa Barbara)
12. Mark Brunell (St. Joseph, Santa Maria)
13. Craig Morton (Campbell)
14. Daryle Lamonica (Clovis)
15. Alex Smith (Helix, La Mesa)
16. Jim Harbaugh (Palo Alto)
17. Steve DeBerg (Savanna, Anaheim)
18. Trent Dilfer (Aptos)
19. Jeff Garcia (Gilroy)
20. Joe Kapp (Hart, Newhall)

Running Backs

1. Marcus Allen (Lincoln, San Diego)
2. O. J. Simpson (Galileo, San Francisco)
3. Ernie Nevers (Santa Rosa)
4. Joe Perry (Jordan, Los Angeles)
5. Ricky Williams (Patrick Henry, San Diego)
6. Marshawn Lynch (Oakland Tech)
7. John Henry Johnson (Pittsburg)

8. Ollie Matson (Washington, San Francisco)
9. Frank Gifford (Bakersfield)
10. Maurice Jones-Drew (De La Salle, Concord)
11. Hugh McElhenny (Washington, Los Angeles)
12. Terrell Davis (Lincoln, San Diego)
13. Freeman McNeil (Banning, Wilmington)
14. Mike Garrett (Roosevelt, Los Angeles)
15. Arian Foster (Mission Bay, San Diego)
16. Reggie Bush (Helix, La Mesa)
17. Dick Bass (Vallejo)
18. Wendell Tyler (Crenshaw, Los Angeles)
19. Glenn Davis (Bonita, La Verne)
20. Charles White (San Fernando)

Receivers

1. James Lofton (Washington, Los Angeles)
2. Lynn Swann (Serra, San Mateo)
3. Steve Smith (University, Los Angeles)
4. Henry Ellard (Hoover, Fresno)
5. Keyshawn Johnson (Dorsey, Los Angeles)
6. Wesley Walker (Carson)
7. Amani Toomer (De La Salle, Concord)
8. Tom Fears (Manual Arts, Los Angeles)
9. Art Powell (San Diego)
10. Anthony Miller (Muir, Pasadena)
11. Curtis Conway (Hawthorne)
12. Gene Washington (Long Beach Poly)
13. DeSean Jackson (Long Beach Poly)
14. Johnnie Morton (South, Torrance)
15. Haven Moses (Lasuen, San Pedro)
16. Tony Hill (Long Beach Poly)
17. Julian Edelman (Woodside)
18. Isaac Curtis (Santa Ana)
19. Webster Slaughter (Franklin, Stockton)
20. Roy Jefferson (Compton)

HIGH SCHOOL FOOTBALL IN CALIFORNIA

Tight Ends

1. Tony Gonzalez (Huntington Beach)
2. Jerry Smith (San Lorenzo)
3. Brent Jones (Leland, San Jose)
4. Delanie Walker (Pomona)
5. Zach Ertz (Monte Vista, Danville)

Offensive Line

1. Anthony Muñoz (Chaffey, Ontario)
2. Larry Allen (Vintage, Napa)*
3. Bruce Matthews (Arcadia)
4. Ron Mix (Hawthorne)
5. Ron Yary (Bellflower)
6. Gary Zimmerman (Walnut)
7. Tyron Smith (Rancho Verde, Moreno Valley)
8. Bob St. Clair (Poly, San Francisco)
9. Ed White (Indio)
10. Logan Mankins (Mariposa County, Mariposa)
11. Don Mosebar (Mt. Whitney, Visalia)
12. Randy Cross (Crespi, Encino)
13. Alex Mack (Dos Pueblos, Goleta)
14. Roy Foster (Taft, Woodland Hills)
15. Lincoln Kennedy (Morse, San Diego)
16. Blaine Nye (Servite, Anaheim)
17. Donald Penn (St. Bernard, Playa del Rey)
18. Aaron Taylor (De La Salle, Concord)
19. Bob Whitfield (Banning, Wilmington)
20. Glenn Parker (Edison, Huntington Beach)

*Last school that he attended; did not play high school football.

Kicker

1. Norm Johnson (Downey)

Punter

1. Bryan Anger (Camarillo)

Defensive Line

1. Gino Marchetti (Antioch)
2. Jared Allen (Los Gatos)
3. La'Roi Glover (Point Loma, San Diego)
4. Charles Mann (Valley, Sacramento)
5. Fred Dryer (Lawndale)
6. Lionel Aldridge (Pittsburg)
7. Jurrell Casey (Long Beach Poly)
8. Andre Carter (Oak Grove, San Jose)
9. Bill McColl (Hoover, San Diego)
10. Manny Fernandez (San Lorenzo)
11. Ben Davidson (Wilson, Los Angeles)
12. Darrell Russell (St. Augustine, San Diego)
13. Kenyon Coleman (Alta Loma)
14. Malik Jackson (Taft, Woodland Hills)
15. Derek Landri (De La Salle, Concord)
16. Regan Upshaw (Pittsburg)
17. Travis Kirschke (Esperanza, Anaheim)
18. Shaun Cody (Los Altos, Hacienda Heights)
19. Jason Fisk (Davis)
20. Erik Howard (Bellarmine Prep, San Jose)

Linebackers

1. Junior Seau (Oceanside)
2. Les Richter (Fresno)
3. Lance Briggs (Elk Grove)
4. Clay Matthews III (Agoura)
5. Ken Norton (Westchester, Los Angeles)
6. Tedy Bruschi (Roseville)
7. Willie McGinest (Long Beach Poly)
8. Joey Porter (Foothill, Bakersfield)

9. Jeff Siemon (Bakersfield)
10. Rod Martin (Hamilton, Los Angeles)
11. Jerry Robinson (Cardinal Newman, Santa Rosa)
12. Jack Del Rio (Hayward)
13. D. J. Williams (De La Salle, Concord)
14. Vontaze Burfict (Centennial, Corona)
15. Marvcus Patton (Leuzinger, Lawndale)
16. Anthony Barr (Loyola, Los Angeles)
17. Malcolm Smith (Taft, Woodland Hills)
18. Jamir Miller (El Cerrito)
19. Kim Bokamper (Milpitas)
20. Fred McNeill (Baldwin Park)

Defensive Backs

1. Ronnie Lott (Eisenhower, Rialto)
2. Mike Haynes (Marshall, Los Angeles)
3. John Lynch (Torrey Pines, San Diego)
4. Jimmy Johnson (Kingsburg)
5. Eric Allen (Point Loma, San Diego)
6. Tim McDonald (Edison, Fresno)
7. Richard Sherman (Dominguez, Compton)
8. Dennis Smith (Santa Monica)
9. Louis Wright (Bakersfield)
10. Nnamdi Asomugha (Narbonne, Harbor City)
11. Mark Carrier (Long Beach Poly)
12. Roy Williams (James Logan, Union City)
13. Chris McAlister (Pasadena)
14. Gill Byrd (Lowell, San Francisco)
15. Eric Turner (Ventura)
16. Brig Owens (Fullerton)
17. Deltha O'Neal (Milpitas)
18. Pat Tillman (Leland, San Jose)
19. Marcus Peters (McClymonds, Oakland)
20. Darryl Lewis (Nogales, La Puente)

Top 20 Winningest Coaches

In California History*

399—Bob Ladouceur, Concord De La Salle, 1979–2012 (24 losses, 3 ties)

360—Marijon Ancich, Santa Fe Springs St. Paul, 1961–1981, 1993–2005, 2009–2011 & Tustin, 1984–1992 (141 losses, 10 ties)

342—Bob Johnson, El Toro, 1979–1990 & Mission Viejo, 1999–2017 (95 losses, 1 tie)

338—Herb Meyer, Oceanside, 1959–1975 & Oceanside El Camino, 1976–2003 (150 losses, 14 ties)

323—John Barnes, Anaheim Magnolia, 1978 & Los Alamitos, 1979–2015 (112 losses, 9 ties)

315—Lou Farrar, Covina Royal Oak, 1983–84 & Covina Charter Oak, 1985–2017 (130 losses, 7 ties) (current)

306—Mike Marrujo, Downey Pius X, 1977–1980 & Placentia Valencia, 1981–2015 (131 losses, 1 tie)

301—Kevin Rooney, Sherman Oaks Notre Dame, 1979–2017 (133 losses, 5 ties) (current)

300—Steve Denman, Tehachapi, 1982–2016 (117 losses, 4 ties) (current)

292—Dick Bruich, Fontana, 1977–1998 & Fontana Kaiser, 2000–2008 (85 losses, 4 ties)

290—Leo Robinson, Woodlake, 1962–2002 (127 losses, 11 ties)

289—Gene Vollnogle, Wilmington Banning, 1957–1962 & Carson, 1963–1990 (73 losses, 1 tie)

287—Mike Herrington, Bellflower 1988 & Newhall Hart, 1989–2017 (83 losses, 2 ties) (current)

284—Bruce Rollinson, Santa Ana Mater Dei, 1989–2017 (83 losses, 2 ties) (current)

282—Mark Loureiro, Escalon, 1989–2017 (67 losses, 1 tie)

280—Mike Janda, San Jose Bellarmine, 1984–2017 (losses, ties not reported) (current)

279—Gary Campbell, Banning, 1969 & Norco, 1970–2003 (115 losses, 4 ties)

274—Randy Blankenship, Grass Valley Nevada Union, 1984–1990 & Fresno Clovis West, 1991–98 & Fallbrook, 1999–2000 & Granbury (Texas), 2001

HIGH SCHOOL FOOTBALL IN CALIFORNIA

& Mission Viejo Capistrano Valley, 2002 & Madera, 2003–08 & Aptos, 2010–17 (96 losses, 6 ties) (current)

273—Jeff Brinkley, Norwalk, 1979–1985 & Newport Beach Newport Harbor, 1986–2017 (177 losses, 7 ties)

270—John Monger, Chino Don Lugo, 1972–1986 & Chino, 1987–2005 (99 losses, 10 ties)

270—Bill Foltmer, Princeton, 1980–1984 & Middletown, 1985–2017 (115 losses, 1 tie) (current)

270—Benny Pierce, Saratoga, 1961–1994 (84 losses, 4 ties)

*Note: 22 are listed, since there is a tie at 270.

Most Consecutive Wins (Team)

151—Concord De La Salle, 1992–2003
61—Modesto Central Catholic, 2001–2005**
48—Westlake Village Oaks Christian, 2003–2007
47—Santa Rosa Cardinal Newman, 1972–1977
46—St. Helena, 1960–1965
46—Temple City, 1969–1973
46—Canyon Country Canyon, 1983–1986
46—Hilmar, 1986–1990
44—Concord De La Salle, 1984–1987
44—San Juan Capistrano St. Margaret's, 2006–09
43—Ventura St. Bonaventure, 1999–2002
42—San Jose Willow Glen, 1958–1962
42—Los Angeles Wilson, 1975–78
41—Mission Viejo, 2001–2003
41—Truckee Tahoe-Truckee, 2009–2012***
40—Concord De La Salle, 2011–2013
39—Bakersfield, 1988–1990
39—Dos Palos, 1997–1999
39—Mission Viejo, 2014–2016
38—Fresno Clovis West, 1992–1994
38—Los Gatos, 2000–2002
38—Perris Citrus Hill, 2007–2009

37—National City Sweetwater, 1983–1985*
36—Willows, 1949–1953
36—San Francisco Poly, 1951–1954
36—Salinas Palma, 1990–1993
35—Los Angeles Loyola, 1962–1964
35—Alameda, 1966–1970
35—Sherman Oaks Notre Dame, 2003–2005
34—Concord De La Salle, 1989–1991

*Forfeits reduced the official streak to 25, 1983–84.
**Plus one win by default.
***California school is member of Nevada state association.
Note: All state records updated throughout each season on Cal-Hi Sports
website (CalHiSports.com)

Players Launched at Nike/Student Sports Events

(Prominent NFL players from California high schools who clearly improved their
college recruiting by attending a Student Sports event in the spring of their
junior year)
LB Vontaze Burfict (Centennial, Corona)
QB Derek Carr (Bakersfield Christian)
WR Brandin Cooks (Lincoln, Stockton)
QB Sam Darnold (San Clemente)
QB Colin Kaepernick (Pitman, Turlock)
RB Marshawn Lynch (Oakland Tech)
OL Alex Mack (San Marcos, Santa Barbara)
RB Doug Martin (St. Mary's, Stockton)
LB Rey Maualuga (Eureka)
WR John Ross (Jordan, Long Beach)
OL Tyron Smith (Rancho Verde, Moreno Valley)

And a Few More Fun Lists

Oldest California High Schools

1851—San Jose Bellarmine

1855—San Francisco St. Ignatius

1856—San Francisco Lowell (August)

1856—Sacramento (Sept.)

1860—California School for the Deaf (North)

1863—San Jose

1863—Berkeley St. Mary's*

1865—Los Angeles Loyola

1867—Petaluma

*Originally in San Francisco.

Geography

Northernmost School: Dorris Butte Valley

Westernmost School: Ferndale

HIGH SCHOOL FOOTBALL IN CALIFORNIA

Southernmost School: San Diego Southwest
Easternmost School: Palo Verde Blythe
Highest School: Mammoth Lakes Mammoth (7000 ft)
Lowest School: Calipatria (184 ft below sea level)

Most Appropriate Player Names

1978—Eddie Fast, Mt. Whitney (Visalia) DB
1971—Travis Hitt, Grossmont (La Mesa) LB
1967—Jim Goforth, Burroughs (Ridgecrest) RB
1952—Larry Wham, San Juan (Fair Oaks) RB
1919—Eddie Sudden, Lick-Wilmerding (San Francisco) Rugby

Most Descriptive Player Names

1979—Rusty Nail, Elk Grove LB-PK
1973—Ernest Dancer, McClymonds (Oakland) OL
1967—Miles Moore, Santa Maria QB
1964—Fair Hooker, Monrovia WR
1963—Rick Shaw, San Diego QB
1942—Teddy Bare, Chino E

Most Unusual Team Nicknames

(Listed in alphabetical order)
Bakersfield Drillers
Bret Harte (Altaville) Bullfrogs
Cathedral (Los Angeles) Phantoms
Coalinga Horned Toads
Chester Volcanoes
Compton Tarbabes
Fremont (Los Angeles) Pathfinders
Glendale Dynamiters
Hollywood Sheiks
Indio Rajahs
Kearny (San Diego) Komets
Lincoln Zebras
Manual Arts (Los Angeles) Toilers

Mayfair (Lakewood) Monsoons
Moorpark Musketeers
Poly (Los Angeles) Parrots
San Benito (Hollister) Haybalers
San Diego Cavers
Stagg (Stockton) Delta Kings
Tustin Tillers
Venice Gondoliers
Vintage (Napa) Crushers
Stockton Tarzans (closed)

Famous Football Alums from California High Schools

(JV, Varsity, & B Levels)
Clint Eastwood (Oakland Tech)
Will Ferrell (University, Irvine)
Mark Harmon (North Hollywood Harvard)
Van Heflin (Long Beach Poly)
Jack Kemp (Fairfax, Los Angeles)
Marion "Suge" Knight (Lynwood)
Al Michaels (Hamilton, Los Angeles)
Gregory Peck (San Diego)
John Raitt (Fullerton)
Fred Savage (Brentwood, Los Angeles)
Tommy Smothers (Redondo, Redondo Beach)
Antonio Villaraigosa (Franklin, Los Angeles)
John Wayne/Marion Morrison (Glendale)
Carl Weathers (Long Beach Poly)
Forest Whitaker (Palisades, Pacific Palisades)
Robin Williams (Redwood, Larkspur)
Brian Wilson (Hawthorne)

Acknowledgments

Any time there is anything produced with the Cal-Hi Sports name on it or if it's something I have produced myself that is centered on high school sports, the person to thank the most is my late uncle, Nelson Tennis. I still think about him every day. He died at age sixty-seven on May 20, 2004, due to complications from bladder cancer. Nelson started compiling California state high school football records in 1975 and expanded it to all sports. We did five printed state record books together and there were two others done after his death based on all of his research. The last one was in 2009 and the goal now is to post everything we can on the website. Nelson probably looked up more than 20,000 state record listings over a nearly 30-year period at the state library in Sacramento.

One of Nelson's best friends and a good friend of mine was Bruce McIntosh, formerly of San Pedro but living in Rio Vista when he died at age eighty-seven on December 1, 2017, in Vacaville. Bruce and Nelson worked together for years helping each other's various projects. I was more than halfway through writing this book when Bruce died. Since then, another project has been to sort through all of Bruce's items. His most prized collection is a vast series of index cards that contains the scores of every California high school football game played from before 1900 to 2009. We'll be doing what we can to spread the news about all of the amazing work that Bruce did.

Bob Barnett of Fresno, the CIF Central Section historian, was another who worked closely with Nelson for many years. Bob continues to supply us with record-breaking achievements from his section. He came through for me as well after I was in a car accident in Madera on my way to see Kazmeir Allen of Tulare break the state touchdown record.

I dedicated this book to my wife Kathleen Moody and my son Sean Tennis, but my parents, George and Joan Tennis of Sacramento, have been instrumental in helping to keep Cal-Hi Sports going during rough years. Eternal gratitude. My other immediate family members have always been there for me too: brother John Tennis, his kids Nelson, Oliver, Penny, and Hattie, cousin Diana Hemme, and great aunt Eleanor Hemme. Eleanor died on March 4, 2018, at age ninety-seven.

They didn't have a role in this book, but since Cal-Hi Sports became a website (CalHiSports.com) in the early 2000s, two who have been invaluable to the process of collecting state records and providing phenomenal content are Ronnie Flores of Norwalk and Harold Abend of Petaluma. Ronnie also has become one of the top boys basketball analysts for team rankings and recruiting in the nation. Harold has concentrated on girls basketball and doesn't miss much when evaluating top players and teams.

Thanks also to another person who has done great work for the site in recent years: Paul Muyskens of Stockton.

Two of the best photographers we've ever worked with have been Willie Eashman of San Francisco and Scott Kurtz of Redondo Beach. Appreciate both of you.

Thanks to everyone who agreed to be interviewed and featured for the various chapters in this book. Some of them are well-known to the California football community. Some are not, but should be.

To my former colleagues at Student Sports and ESPN: We had some magical years together, and I hope to see you all soon. Thanks especially to former publishing partner Andy Bark, with whom I worked for 25 years from the middle of the 1980s to 2012.

Thanks as well to those I've gotten to know well in the California prep sports media community, who continue to do great work despite horrendous cutbacks in staffing that are ravaging many media companies. I mentioned Eric Sondheimer of the *Los Angeles Times* in the introduction. Appreciation as well to Joe Davidson of the *Sacramento Bee*, Mitch Stephens of MaxPreps and *The San Francisco Chronicle*, Kevin Askeland of MaxPreps, Chace Bryson of *SportStars Magazine*, John Maffei and Steve Brand of *The San Diego Union-Tribune*, Steve Fryer and Dan Albano of the *Orange County Register*, Eric-Paul Johnson of *The Press-Enterprise* (Riverside), Rich Estrada of Black Hat Football, Darren Sabedra of the *San Jose Mercury-News*, Jim Crandell of FOX40 in Sacramento, Robert Braunstein of the 49ers Cal-Hi Sports Report, Trevor Horn of the *Bakersfield Californian*, Thomas Lawrence and Scott Linesburgh of *The Record* (Stockton), Joe Cortez and

James Burns of *The Modesto Bee*, Andy Boogaard formerly of *The Fresno Bee*, Evan Barnes formerly of the *Los Angeles Daily News*, Carlos Arias of SoCalSidelines.com, and Mike Guardabascio, formerly of the *Long Beach Press-Telegram*.

I'd be remiss not to mention those from the California Interscholastic Federation and many from the CIF section offices who have given Cal-Hi Sports great professional courtesy over the years. This includes executive director Roger Blake, associate executive director Ron Nocetti, communications director Rebecca Brutlag, and section media relations directors Thom Simmons (CIF Southern Section) and Will DeBoard (CIF Sac-Joaquin Section).

Finally, thanks to all the players and coaches from California schools I've had the pleasure of watching since going to my first game with Nelson and my father in 1969. I think it was a Nevada Union (Grass Valley) game in Roseville. I've felt something special about Friday nights in the fall ever since.